"*Learning to Be* is the book many of us have been wa[iting for...au]thenticity come through on every page. This is a boo[k not only about] learning to be, but also learning to heal and thrive. You [tell the story] of learning to love yourself fully and embrace the love of God deeply. More than once I found myself reading and saying, 'Yes that's me too. Thank you for letting me know I'm not alone, thank you for using your own story and the lessons learned to offer the rest of us a roadmap.' In *Learning to Be* you will be affirmed on the journey to be authentically you, whole and healed."

Romal Tune, author of *Love Is an Inside Job: Getting Vulnerable with God*

"Every perfectionist should read this book, every Southern 'good girl,' every person who has ever felt empty. 'The reality is, many of us stand in a circle with stones in hand all too often,' says Pastor Rasmus. Then she convinces us, her readers, to set down our stones."

Andrea White, novelist and civic leader

"Juanita and I have been friends for many years. I admire her preaching and teaching gifts, and value her generous contribution as a member of our Renovaré ministry team. Juanita describes herself as a type A personality. This is indeed true . . . although triple A might be a little more accurate description! Her 'crash,' as she describes her major depressive episode, was exactly that in every sense—physical, mental, emotional, and spiritual. I say all this to underscore for you the importance of *Learning to Be*. This is a book of genuine substance dealing with the most heart-wrenching needs of the human soul. *Learning to Be* is an essential resource for every person seeking to navigate life in contemporary culture. I recommend it highly."

Richard J. Foster, author of *Celebration of Discipline* and *Sanctuary of the Soul*

"Carl Rodgers wrote, 'That which is most personal is most universal.' *Learning to Be* by Juanita Rasmus is a book of autobiographical vulnerability about her 'crash' with a depressive mood disorder. In her candid reflection she creates a psycho/spiritual worldview that is a resource for us all. This is a must-read for all who seek to find a faith that is both practical and functional, a nonsentimental spirituality."

J. Pittman McGehee, Episcopal priest and author of *The Paradox of Love*

"We live in the two worlds of doing and being. Juanita's 'crash' was perhaps a clash of these two worlds. This book is a bold record of how she handled 'the crash.' Her lull allowed her to not only slow down but to go deep inside where literary giant Alice Walker says that we find God. Once deep inside, Juanita embraced and reflected on spiritual disciplines that provided a healing path for her. Her examples and stories facilitate a path for our own growth and invite us to not only embrace spiritual disciplines but to celebrate them so that ultimately we can learn to write our own ode to something or someone as our spiritual exercise."

Dr. Henry L. Masters Sr., publisher of *By Faith Magazine* and author of *Makin' Room in the Inn: African American Christian Hospitality*

"A real learning to be book. Beginning with her experience of depression, the author offers us a rich guide to helpful resources and Christian practice that will enable readers to grow and to appreciate more deeply who they really are. An excellent guide for a dark time."

Sr. Mary Dennison, Cenacle Spiritual Direction Institute

"From the moment I began Juanita's very personal and beautifully written story, I could not put it down. She speaks deep truth on every page as she recounts what caused her 'crash,' and how she found her true identity as the beloved child of God she is. This book describes a life-giving journey—a journey to authentic freedom—that all of us need to hear."

James Bryan Smith, author of *The Good and Beautiful God*

"With grace and courage, Juanita Rasmus invites the reader to follow her journey from what she calls 'the crash'—her own dark night of the soul—through her valley of facing her own shadow, self-doubt, perfectionism, depression, and fear, to the encounter with her true self. Not as an exhibitionist but as an authentic seeker, Juanita beams the light of hope on our own valleys and midlife crises as well as on the possibilities and processes of rebirth, recovery, restoration, and transformation. Juanita's story is a story of faith at work, walking the talk, persistence, and patience. By telling her story, Juanita shows us that it is possible to walk through our own valleys, not getting stuck in them but allowing God to use the raw and rough edges of our lives for good."

Jeanie Miley, author, retreat leader, spiritual director, and Bible study teacher

"We have always misunderstood and misrepresented mental health, especially in women. Juanita's book reads as a real conversational model to engage health in a very meaningful way. Juanita's inward journey reflects her ability to rely upon and use the spiritual teachings and strong religious foundation that are core to her life. These are two key elements of any in-depth journey into the discovery of one's true self. Juanita also provides guidance and direction in approaching the journey to self, sharing her own journey in such a way that anyone using the book can feel accompanied and lovingly supported. I loved this book and felt embraced by the gift of a friend sharing her spiritual journey."

Myokei Caine-Barrett, Shonin, resident priest at the Myoken-ji Temple, Houston, bishop of the Nichiren Shu Order of North America

"Each of us will experience pain and loss throughout our lives, and the names that we designate for the ways in which we may suffer are many. We can only hope that those who endure the descent possess both the desire to share their story and the words to communicate the details of their depths. With an arduously earned presence born, in part, through a personal commitment to hold the hands of those in need as they struggle and seek to understand a new reality, Pastor Juanita Rasmus possesses both the story and the words. Throughout her book, the reader joins with her to laugh and marvel, to wonder and contemplate, to pause and recognize the fragility of our lives. Stories from those who have sustained the dark night serve as a reminder and guide rail as we all confront dark nights of our own. I feel thankful that her voice and story now rest in the recesses of my heart, for I know I will call upon them one day."

John W. Price, host of *The Sacred Speaks* and cofounder of the Center for the Healing Arts and Sciences

"Pastor Juanita Rasmus has written a winsome, raw, and powerful narrative about her unique story—her own mental health crash. And yet even as it is her story, it is one that will resonate with all of us, especially in these times as we have been pushed to breaking. *Learning to Be* should be read by anyone who struggles to know how God and community matter when life is hard, really all of us. I was changed by reading this book."

Elaine Howard Ecklund, Herbert S. Autrey Chair in Social Sciences at Rice University and author of *Why Science and Faith Need Each Other*

JUANITA
CAMPBELL RASMUS

LEARNING

TO

FINDING YOUR CENTER
AFTER THE BOTTOM
FALLS OUT

FOREWORD BY
Tina Knowles Lawson

An imprint of InterVarsity Press
Downers Grove, Illinois

InterVarsity Press
P.O. Box 1400 | Downers Grove, IL 60515-1426
ivpress.com | email@ivpress.com

InterVarsity Press® is the publishing division of InterVarsity Christian Fellowship/USA®. For more information, visit intervarsity.org.

All Scripture quotations, unless otherwise indicated, are taken from The Holy Bible, New International Version®, NIV®. Copyright © 1973, 1978, 1984, 2011 by Biblica, Inc.™ Used by permission of Zondervan. All rights reserved worldwide. www.zondervan.com. The "NIV" and "New International Version" are trademarks registered in the United States Patent and Trademark Office by Biblica, Inc.™

While any stories in this book are true, some names and identifying information may have been changed to protect the privacy of individuals.

The publisher cannot verify the accuracy or functionality of website URLs used in this book beyond the date of publication.

Cover design: David Fassett
Interior design: Daniel van Loon
Images: abstract watercolor: ©Sergey Ryumin/Moment Collection/Getty Images
         colorful watercolor: ©licccka/iStock/Getty Images Plus

ISBN 978-1-5140-0382-4 (print) | ISBN 978-0-8308-4386-2 (digital)

Printed in the United States of America ♾

Library of Congress Cataloging-in-Publication Data
Names: Rasmus, Juanita Campbell, 1961- author.
Title: Learning to be : finding your center after the bottom falls out / Juanita Campbell Rasmus.
Description: Downers Grove, Illinois : IVP, an imprint of InterVarsity Press, 2020. | Includes bibliographical references.
Identifiers: LCCN 2020008009 (print) | LCCN 2020008010 (ebook) | ISBN 9780830845873 (hardcover) I ISBN 9780830843862 (ebook)
Subjects: LCSH: Depression, Mental–Religious aspects–Christianity. | Mental health–Religious aspects–Christianity. | Depressed persons–Religious life.
Classification: LCC BV4910.34 .R37 2020 (print) | LCC BV4910.34 (ebook) | DDC 248.8/6–dc23
LC record available at https://lccn.loc.gov/2020008009
LC ebook record available at https://lccn.loc.gov/2020008010

30 29 28 27 26 25 24 23 | 13 12 11 10 9 8 7 6 5 4 3 2 1

To my family unnamed and named,
some through blood,
some through choice,
all in love.

Leonard

Florence

Elischa

Rudy

Mildred

Rudolph (posthumously)

Morgan

Ryan

Hamilton

Mary

Henry

Jaden

Baby Harris

I Love You.

And to you dear reader!
Thank you.

CONTENTS

FOREWORD

Tina Knowles Lawson

To give light to those who sit in darkness and in the shadow
of death, to guide our feet into the way of peace.

Luke 1:79 NRSV

*L*uke 1:79 speaks of God's mercy shining on us in times of great darkness, a light strong enough and bright enough to guide our feet toward peace.

I've experienced this light in my faith walk and with powerful, resilient people like Juanita Campbell Rasmus, a woman I met in 1986 when I opened my first salon, and she became a faithful client. She set an example for the power of prayer and worship, and I later became one of the first members of St. John's Church.

Over the years, I've witnessed Juanita navigate the highs and lows of marriage, motherhood, ministry, and womanhood. I've seen her journey from the self-professed "good girl" to a leader who wholeheartedly seeks God with a level of authenticity, transparency, and grace that is unmatched. And in this book, she inspires us to do the same.

In *Learning to Be*, Juanita invites us into one of the most intimate and revealing spaces of her life, which was her battle with depression—"the crash."

Juanita doesn't close the door or sugarcoat her episode. Instead, it's an eye-opening and entertaining read that encourages us to navigate from our own version of "the crash" and discover what an authentic relationship with ourselves and God looks like as we shed the pretenses and walk in God's infinite light.

We aren't meant to dwell in the dark. But darkness can be an indicator helping us to ask the tough questions and take one faithful step at a time toward being all God created us to be. I can't imagine another person I'd want to usher me through such an intimate and raw journey. I'm thankful that a book like this exists. Whatever brings you to this book, I pray that it will bless you on your journey.

1

THE STRESS OF LIVING IN
A DO-DO-DO WORLD

*I*t felt as though every nerve in my body was popping. Imagine large, strong hands slowly applying pressure to a family-sized package of uncooked spaghetti noodles. I was the spaghetti. Breaking down one piece at a time.

It was a morning like any other. On August 27, I got up and cooked breakfast for my husband, Rudy, and our daughters, Morgan and Ryan. The school year had just started, and the girls were excited. I called them to the table, and as they sat down, I rushed to the bathroom to put on my makeup before I took them to school.

"Hey, I'll take the girls this morning," Rudy volunteered.

"Great!" I told him. "That'll give me a few more minutes to get ready so I can finish my makeup in the restroom instead of the rearview mirror." We laughed.

Rudy and the girls finished breakfast, and we all said goodbye with our usual hugs and I love yous. I finished putting on my makeup and then opened the bathroom door to leave. Without warning, a horrible wave of nausea swept over me like a bad flu. I felt so sick I could hardly walk or think straight. I'd never felt anything like it before, but I knew I couldn't go anywhere that morning. I called the office of St. John's Church and asked our secretary to reschedule my early appointments.

"If I lay down for a couple of hours, I'm sure I'll feel better and be in this afternoon," I told her.

Minutes later, however, I had an uneasy feeling that something was happening to me. I watched my hand pick up the phone as if I lacked control over it and hit the redial button. When my secretary answered, I mumbled almost incoherently, "I'm not feeling well, and I don't know when I'll be back. I'm taking a leave of absence or medical leave or a sabbatical or something." And I hung up the phone. I struggled back to bed and lay there feeling like every nerve in me was short-circuiting.

Days passed with me in bed, overwhelmed by a sensation of falling, spiraling, and spinning into a pitch-black tunnel day after bleak day. I felt sheer panic as I tried reaching out to grab something—anything!—to stop my fall, but my hands found nothing to hold on to. The feeling was so intense, all I could do was hope that I would finally hit bottom.

I Never Saw It Coming

Around our house that awful day is called "the crash." Now that I have had time to reflect, I realize that it had a catalyst. A complex mix of stress, disappointment, grief, compassion fatigue, vicarious trauma, and discouragement had been building up for weeks, months, and years, but I discounted the warning signs.

Most summers, Morgan and Ryan were involved in all kinds of activities. For some reason the summer of the crash was different. Normally, my summer workday ended at 3 p.m., which allowed me to pick up the girls from camp or wherever they were. That summer, however, the girls came to church with my husband and me every day.

I served as copastor with Rudy. We basically split the responsibilities down the middle along our lines of interest and giftedness. I was teaching two Bible studies a week and preaching every other Sunday, and I was responsible for women's ministry, spiritual formation, and pastoral conversations with the women. Additionally, I served as the head of public relations for the Bread of Life, our nonprofit organization that provided a daily meal to the homeless community we served in the church.

The girls had learned to pack their books and toys when they accompanied us to work. That summer they made beaded bracelets and necklaces that they sold to the business people who attended the Wednesday noon Bible study. In addition to their coloring and crafts, the girls learned basic office tasks like helping to fold bulletins and found creative ways to occupy themselves. Instead of leaving in the afternoon to spend time at home with them, I thought, *This is the best of both worlds. The girls are with us, and we can stay at church and get more work done.* It was the perfect arrangement for a performance-addicted perfectionist!

Many times our family would run out for a quick dinner and then return to the church to work. When we finally returned home each night, Rudy and I often would talk about issues at the church. Then we would get up the next morning and put in another ten- or twelve-hour day.

Our church was growing at a rate of about five hundred people per year. (We had started the church with nine members.) Rudy and I had served this three-thousand-member congregation for years. We had no idea how understaffed we were or the toll it took on us individually and as a young family. We had a handful of committee volunteers who helped us to keep the wheels on the bus, so to speak.

I often felt exhausted not just from the work but also from the emotional trauma that I experienced vicariously through meeting with parishioners and hearing their stories. Vicarious trauma is like secondhand smoke—it can be deadly to those exposed to it. Two years before the crash, two very dear friends had died. Both times I rose to the occasion with my self-proclaimed vow: *I have to be strong for them, and then I can fall apart.* To this day I have no idea what gave me that notion, but I didn't take the time to process the pain. In fact, I had never allowed myself to grieve any of the losses I'd experienced, whether deaths, business setbacks, failures, broken relationships, or other disappointments. My way of coping with pain was to stuff it and keep moving.

Clearly, we were not caring for ourselves in life-giving ways. We were sleep deprived, ate too many fast-food meals, and depended on caffeinated drinks to give us a boost to keep going. All of these factors, I later learned, were "lifestyle deficiencies" that would catch up to us sooner or later. Still, I loved what I was doing. What was the problem with doing a little extra work for the Lord? I loved God and I loved the ministry. God calls us to sacrifice, right?

Meet the Good Girl

Up to that point, my life had been rooted in the biblical model of the virtuous woman found in Proverbs 31 and the belief that I needed to be picture perfect. I had to be the flawless wife, the impeccable mother, and the textbook pastor. My whole identity was to be a "good girl" who always did the right thing and pleased the people around me. Nothing less was acceptable to me. Doing the right thing meant living by rules. If I couldn't figure out what the rules were in a situation, I created my own rules to live by that would keep me on the perfect path of righteousness.

My personality is type A, high performing. Yet the price of my drivenness was my physical and emotional health. Forty years of buried feelings and pent-up stress caused everything to come crashing down that morning. It was as though I had built my life on a foundation of toothpicks. I lacked the tools to deal with the inevitable bumps and bruises of life, and I allowed the pressure to escalate until damage was inevitable.

I related to Martha when she said to Jesus, "Lord, don't you care that my sister has left me to do the work by myself? Tell her to help me!" (Luke 10:40). The mantra "Good girls don't get mad" played incessantly in my head. I had set such a high bar of accomplishment and perfection for myself that I often swallowed my anger at my own imperfection and the imperfection of those around me. I was angry that I was working so hard and it didn't seem to matter, no one seemed to notice, and there was no one to celebrate my good and hard work. My anger was undercover, or so I thought. And even though I wouldn't admit to the anger, my body knew. The anger showed up as pounding headaches, stomach problems, and backaches that the doctor called sciatica. I called it a pain in the assets. It all seemed to come out of nowhere.

My emotions were like beach balls in a swimming pool. I would push them under the water, but if I let go, all that pressure and energy sent the balls to the surface and flying out of the pool with rocketlike force. I was holding down a lot of balls.

Friends and family reflected on how wound up I was. Relationships suffered—I didn't have time to "waste" talking to friends about getting together. I had things to do and places to go. Though I valued my friendships, my to-do list took priority over my to-be list. I was running on empty. And since I was meeting my deadlines, for the most part, I never noticed the growing problem.

A Journey Together

In the 1500s Saint John of the Cross wrote a mystical poem describing the "dark night of the soul," and this season was my version of that dark night. The dark night is an invitation to enter into the mystery of our unknowing, both the unknowing of ourselves and the unknowing of God. It invites us to know and be fully known to ourselves and to know God in ways that perhaps we had never imagined. The dark night was for me the beginning of freedom.

In the chapters to come I invite you to enter into my journey. I'll explore how I arrived at this place, how things grew worse, and the spiritual practices that brought me to the other side. In each chapter I have included questions to help you reflect on your own journey or tips to help you assess where you are.

I chose to share my story because all too often in Western culture, and especially in the church, we are reticent to discuss mental health along with the related spiritual implications. It is my hope that telling my story will shed light on the resources available to someone in the aftermath of a mental health diagnosis (or any devastation that affects one's well-being) and provide courage to wait in the darkness, because often that's where the real treasures are stored.

Even with such a diagnosis, we can learn to live into new realities that bring freedom and may even make learning to live with the disaster or diagnosis worth the descent into hell. Like the phoenix rising from the ashes, we too can rise as we discover ways of *being* in a world driven by *doing*.

PAUSE TO REFLECT

St. Ignatius of Loyola, founder of the Jesuits, also experienced a life-altering illness and its accompanying revelations. During his year of conversion Ignatius began to write insights that later would be called the *Spiritual Exercises*. Ignatius believed that the chief need in the busy world of Rome was a daily tool to observe or to pay attention to one's life, and his *Exercises* teach the practice of examen. I offer the "Pause to Reflect" at the end of each chapter as a means of inviting you to stop briefly and reflect on what may be roused as you move through my story. As Socrates noted, "An unexamined life is not worth living."

I encourage you to practice the examen as you read this book by reflecting each day in a journal or perhaps on your phone by asking yourself, *What gave me life, awakened me, or moved me in this reading or during the day? or How did I experience love?* Jot it down. Next ask, *What challenged me, left me puzzled, or stirred me? Where did I feel the absence of love?* Jot it down. Then, after reflecting on both, give thanks for the awareness that each offered. One of the gifts of reflection is the invitation to do more of what gives you life and less of the things that are not life-giving.

Have you or someone you loved experienced depression or a mental health diagnosis?

What beliefs did you have about yourself or the person with the diagnosis?

As you journal and experience your awareness, notice any stigmas or preconceived ideas you may have about mental health illnesses. Stay open to new ways of seeing as you move through this journey of learning to *be*.

2

WHO AM I?

Over the next months, as I lay flat on my back in the midst of the darkness and the silence, the Holy Spirit gently asked me, *Who are you?* I would have laughed had I been in my normal mind, yet the question was so poignant it pierced through me like a hot knife cutting through butter.

I almost said, "Well if you don't know who I am, and I don't know who I am, then Houston, we have a problem!" I wanted to say, "I am Rudy's wife; I am Morgan and Ryan's mother," and run down a list of the roles I play in other relationships, but at that moment I knew that it might be wise to toss the question back to God to gain some real clarity.

God was present in the question; I was sure of that. Who am I? There is the story I had been telling myself of my identity, the story my parents had told me, the story my grandparents had told me, the story I learned of myself while I was in elementary school, and the story the neighborhood kids and my cousins told me. It was amazing that I hadn't combusted before then from all the internal contradictions. I had way too many accounts of the Juanita story, so it's no wonder why I was clueless as to how to answer the question.

Searching for Identity

Do we ever really know who we are? Wouldn't it be great to be asked while growing up, "Who are you, really?" This question could be followed by having God reveal the answer to that question in a thunderous announcement so that by the time we hit thirty we would have some practice being ourselves and could be a little more self-assured.

There is something extremely disorienting in discovering that you don't know yourself. During this period, I was having conversations with God that went something like this: *If knowing myself is supposed to be a divine revelation, okay, I'm good with that. But c'mon, God. If you could go to all the trouble of having a placenta delivered after a baby's birth, then why not attach a little note: This is Juanita, she is my beloved and she is . . . !* This revelation I longed for from God would feel like the surprise you get when you or a friend are told the gender of a long-awaited baby. Unfortunately, it doesn't work that way. For me, the crash provided an opportunity to reveal my identity.

Pastor Myles Monroe said, "If you want to know the purpose of a thing, never ask the thing, ask the manufacturer." That phrase stuck with me. He further said that when we don't know the purpose of a thing, abuse is inevitable. I can see that in my life, especially now. I see it in my failure to recognize the necessity of rest, proper nutrition, and exercise. I see it in the many ways that I abused my body, mind, and spirit. I had no idea that I could destroy my life by pure ignorance.

Lying flat on my back for days on end gave me plenty of time to reflect on the choices that seemed expedient at the time but had long-term negative effects. It's downright ignorance, like ignoring the warning lights flashing on my car dashboard while I keep driving. How much of this could have been avoided? Who really cared if I burned the candle on both ends? The spoken and unspoken demands on my time and energy were unyielding, so it seemed. Everywhere I turned, somebody wanted something from me.

Every person or organization I was associated with wanted something from me. Our congregation had grown so rapidly that I was receiving more "opportunities" to serve and speak, and the requests seemed endless. Teachers wanted my kids at school on time, homework in hand, and I seemed to have a flexible schedule, so "Mrs. Rasmus, could you go on the field trip tomorrow?" or "Could you volunteer to help us with the science fair this year?" Directors of after-school activity programs wanted me to turn in the money from the candy sale that supported their work. My church wanted me, and I thought that I needed to be available to the church—no limits, no holds barred. So I gave my life over to my job because, after all, I work for *God*.

It isn't that any one of these expectations and requests were unreasonable or unpleasurable; the problem was that all too often I had been finding my identity in doing all this stuff, and so I felt obligated to say yes to everything. I had not developed the ability to set boundaries or have realistic expectations for myself.

HALT

My friend Regina Hassan has made a career of coaching folks in sobriety. She likes to use the acronym HALT to help people gauge when they are putting themselves at risk of relapse. According to Regina, when we find ourselves too *hungry*, too *angry*, too *lonely*, or too *tired*, we need to halt! In my case, paying attention to these could have helped me see I was in danger of having my life spin out of control.

But anger is sneaky, at least for me, because good girls never want to admit that they are angry in the first place. And, of course, we would *never* be resentful. So, I tried to be cool, calm, and collected though I resented the infrequent suggestions of friends, family, or even a coworker or two that my life was out of whack. But it was. It may have looked good on the outside, high functioning and all, but I had begun to fall apart on the inside.

Regina taught me another acronym for the word *denial*: Don't Even Know I Am Lying. When we look at our lives, it is so easy to find fault and want to point fingers. Too often I have heard kids blame their parents while denying that they (the kids) had made choices that created the problems they were now having to live with. I see this frequently in my role as a pastor as I listen to people tell their stories. In many cases there is some level of denial going on unless the person has started to deconstruct their childhood story with a healthy dose of grace and truth.

I, too, slipped into the river of denial and blamed my parents for certain things about my childhood rather than acknowledging I had created a false narrative about it. In all honesty, my parents, like so many others, only did what they knew to do, and I totally get it, because that's what I'm doing now as a parent. We work with the tools we have, no matter how our kids perceive the tools.

Many times I had preached that when we point the finger of blame, there are always three fingers pointing back at us. While that was a great preaching point, it didn't feel nearly as clever when it applied to my own life. At its core, blaming is a sign that there is brokenness that needs to be healed. I am clear that my crash and its results were not about my parents but about finding out who I was down deep beneath the story that I had constructed about my life—a story of denial and blame, a story that only I could edit and transform.

God has the most incredible ways of revealing our brokenness. But God wasn't done yet.

No, Not the Prodigal, I'm the Other One

Just a couple of months before the crash, I read the story of the prodigal son (Luke 15:11-32) as I prepared for a sermon. I meditated on the text for a week; there was so much in it that unnerved me. I had always understood the parable as the story of a son who had taken his share of the family wealth. Over time and due to his immaturity, he had carelessly spent what should have been his inheritance.

I didn't identify with this guy at all. I was furious—how dare he make unnecessary demands on his parents and fly the coop, leaving his brother to take care of the parents and the payments on the indebted estate and abandoning his brother to run the family business alone.

In contrast, I identified with the brother who stayed home. He was the responsible one. In school growing up, my identity was tied to being the responsible one. When my grandmother needed a chore done, I did it. So I related to the brother who was stuck at home.

What I hadn't noticed before but see now is that the older brother had been so busy working and being responsible that he had not allowed himself to really live, to find his identity, apart from his ability to perform. No doubt he saw himself as the successful one—dependable, wise, mature. Perhaps in his own head he was the favored one, the perfect child, anxious to be esteemed and praised.

According to psychiatrist Murray Bowen's family systems theory, each person in a family plays a role. Someone is the hero, while other family members may be a scapegoat, a lost child, or a mascot. Based on this theory, the guy in the parable who stayed home would probably identify himself as a hero—strong, superior, busy, conservative, and trustworthy. For the first time I became aware of the attitude that had been building in this brother. The resemblance was unnervingly close to home.

As my revelation continued, I realized that the parable wasn't about one prodigal son but rather two, the younger one who left home to discover himself and the older one who played it safe, too focused on doing the "good" thing at the cost of discovering himself. The older brother and I had more in common than I cared to admit.

PAUSE TO REFLECT

The crash became an opportunity for self-discovery, an invitation to uncover my identity beyond the ideas formed in my childhood, which was so rooted in doing. What story have you been telling yourself? In the story of the prodigal son, which brother do you most identify with? Or is there a historical story that you find sheds light on your childhood sense of identity? Perhaps it would interest you to look into Bowen's family systems theory for insight about the role you played in your family system.

The crash has caused me to question my story about my identity. Byron Katie has developed a process called "The Work" that uses four questions to invite inquiry into the myths we have been living with and projecting onto ourselves and others: (1) Is it true? (2) Is it really true? (3) How do you respond? (4) Who would you be without that thought?

Allow yourself permission to sit in this story and to breathe it in: live into it, try it on for size. What do you notice as you cast yourself in the lineup of characters? What insights are made available to you? What shift or insight occurs for you?

Interlude

AN ODE TO THE
PRODIGAL BROTHER

While I lay in bed I gave myself permission to imagine being the older brother in the ancient story of the prodigal son and what that might feel and sound like. How would it feel to move beyond anger, resentment, and denial to a place of compassion for the younger brother who left home? What would it feel like to honor the younger brother's courage and his response to the call to discover his truest self? I gave myself permission to sit in this story and to breathe it in and to live into it. "Ode to the Prodigal Brother" is the result of my musings.

Little brother, please forgive me.
I just didn't understand.
I didn't understand that the call to find yourself
caused you to create havoc back at the house.
I didn't understand that the call to become
who you thought you ultimately needed to be
called you to risk everything
to be free.

I didn't understand.
I didn't understand that while I was trapped
in my own mind, in my own heart,
you had found the courage
to unbuckle the straps that kept you bound.
That kept you bound to home and what that meant
to you.
Forgive me. I just didn't understand.
I didn't understand that there was a call in you that
meant
you had to go; you had no choice.
And if that meant burning bridges, settling estates,
and selling properties to get your freedom ticket,
you had to go.
You had to,
to live.
Forgive me.
I just didn't understand.
I didn't understand what it was
that would cause you to turn our home upside down,
to leave me with the parents, the business, and the
debt.
I just didn't understand.
And so, I ask today that you would forgive me for
all the times
I cursed you, wished you a fated ill.
For all the times I wondered
and sometimes even still wonder.

I now realize that you had to leave.
You had to go.
It was the only way that you would come to know
who you were,
the son of your father,
and where you would find your life
within his warm embrace.
So, forgive me. I never had the courage to leave,
never had the courage to strike out and be free
(know freedom).
Never knew what it was
to be me.
Never knew what it was to come home
to the full love of a father who had been waiting
all along,
Open arms
Bright smile
Robe for my back
Ring for my hand.
The honored guest of my own party.
Forgive me.
I never knew you had to surrender it all to be
totally emptied
so that you could come to a place of being totally
filled.
Forgive me. I just didn't know.

3

THE HOLLOW BUNNY RULES

As a child, rules kept me safe from judgment and harm, safe from breaking any of God's do-not-cross-this-line rules. I thought the rules worked: I didn't drink, I didn't smoke, I didn't steal, I didn't gamble, I didn't . . . and so on, my little checklist of righteousness went.

And yet I was aware that my life had a certain quality of hollowness to it. With all the time on my hands during the crash, I reflected on how often I felt as though I was just going through the motions of life. I felt empty inside, as though nothing about my life was filling me up, filling up the essential self. I was busy but not always present; so many things I did were by rote. Too many of my days before the moment of the crash felt like the mechanical wind-up bunny on the battery commercial just going through the motions beating my lil' drum, or the idealized playboy bunnies from the 2004 science-fiction movie remake *The Stepford Wives*. In the movie the wives live identical lives based on programming designed to please their husbands. Their lives were monotonous, efficient, stylish, perfect, boring, plastic, and empty. Those women had no thoughts or ideas of their own. My perception of needing to be perfect had left me as hollow as these wives. Somehow I had lost something, or perhaps I had just run out of something like wonder, awe, excitement, spontaneity, or adventure. Perfection sucks the life out of us without any advanced warning, and all we are left with is the empty container.

I had a great husband and wonderful daughters, but something in me felt empty. When our lives have been built on perfectionism and rule following that no longer serve us, we are left with a sense of hollowness and sadness. Before the crash I wouldn't allow my mind to dwell on that hollowness too long because I worried that it would cause my life to spiral downward to a place I dared not even wonder about. Yet in the back of my mind there was the unspoken question, *Is this all there is and then you die?* I had no one I felt I could talk to about this, nor did I really have a language to convey what I was feeling. Heck, I was the pastor—wasn't *I* suppose to have all the answers?

Discovering I Was a Hollow Bunny

My life leading up to the crash seemed hollow like the chocolate bunnies sold at Easter time. Many of the bunnies are in beautiful boxes and have the appearance of a solid chocolate bunny. They all look equally attractive. But when we bite into one that's hollow, we immediately discover the emptiness inside. I was a hollow bunny, though I didn't yet understand why. But understanding began to come to me one day while I was lying on the sofa in the living room a few days after the crash.

The room was filled with the warm midday sun. As I lay there, the Lord said, *You have built a life filled with rules. Your rules have boxed you in, and they have boxed me out.*

I didn't get it. Wasn't the God-life all about following rules? Isn't Christianity rooted in *Thou shalt not?* Had I gotten what it meant to be a Christian totally wrong? If it wasn't about the rules, then what had I wasted my time and life doing all these years? And if I had gotten this all wrong, what else had I gotten wrong about God? Even more, what would it take to get it right?

I sat with this word from the Lord for quite a long time.

My New Fortune

Many evenings while I was recovering, Rudy was left to sort out dinner. On one particular night he brought home Chinese food. Our family has a habit when we have Chinese food of reading the fortunes from the fortune cookies out loud. So that night at the end of the meal we each read our fortunes. Mine said, "Rules without relationship equals rebellion." I read it several times because it felt worth repeating. I thought, *This will be a motto that underlines our parenting from this day forward.* So I went to the refrigerator, grabbed a magnet, and attached the fortune at eye level on the freezer door. I wanted to make sure I wouldn't miss this valuable message for raising our girls.

As time went on, however, and as I saw that fortune day after day, God began to make clear that it was really meant for me, was really about me. God used the fortune-cookie note to un-ravel my misunderstanding of the purpose of rules and to lead me to finding freedom from my addiction to rules and the box I had placed myself in as a child. In the process I began to expe-rience freedom in my relationship with God and joy that I had never known. I came to see that my childhood rules rooted in the Ten Commandments, Sunday school lessons, and midweek services all had a place. The problem was that I had put them in first place as a child and had never revisited their priority in my life. I had made rules my god.

I now see that the rules were meant to be like training wheels on a kid's first bicycle. They were there to help me learn to balance myself, to offer support until I could ride by my own power, under my own authority.

I remember the day my daddy and I talked about taking the training wheels off my first bike. While the thought was a little scary, it also felt like it was time. Daddy guided me down Brill Street, in Houston's Fifth Ward, and helped me stay steady by holding the seat of my pink bike until I got used to riding without the training wheels. Along the way Daddy coached me, saying, "Peddle, Juanita. Hold the bars, Juanita."

Before I knew it, he had let go of my seat, and I rode, a little wobbly at first, but under my own power—one rooted in freedom. I wasn't alone. Daddy was present. But I no longer needed the training wheels because I had my own power and my daddy's presence to secure me and his voice to guide me.

Rules alone had left me hollow inside, but the sense that the Spirit was freeing me to be in relationship was so life-giving that all I could call it was joy. Something about this new awareness began to fill some of the emptiness that I had been feeling. If we are living solely by the rules, we become like the hollow chocolate Easter bunnies. I have found that relationship with God and my practice of abiding with God, being joined with God, are what make me solid inside and out. I was becoming a chocolate bunny filled with good stuff, like chocolate ganache or something rich and surprisingly wonderful. Perhaps the word *love* best describes what seemed to be flowing into me; yes, a deep knowing that I was loved.

This rules-without-relationship-equals-rebellion lesson taught me about the power of relationship and the freedom that the Spirit offers us and—dare I say—longs for us to know. God is all about relationship, the intimacy of knowing and being known. I had never imagined God was longing for me to take off the training wheels—the rules and my childhood notions that were keeping me from knowing my own power and freedom—to be in relationship with my authentic self and especially with God.

PAUSE TO REFLECT

The mystical poem "Dark Night of the Soul" by Saint John of the Cross refers to the laborious experience of being emptied out as purgation, active purification. He explains that the process is guided by God to prepare the individual to be in union with love. St. John writes, "God brings it [the soul] into the passive purgation of the dark night whereof. . . . It befits the soul, however to contrive to labour, in so far as it can, on its own account, to the end that it may purge and perfect itself, and thus may merit being taken by God into that Divine care wherein it becomes healed of all things that it was unable of itself to cure." My attachment to rules was the thing I needed to be cured of. Seeing the fortune helped bring that reality to consciousness, but it was God's gentle presence, like my father guiding me after the training wheels came off, that gave me my autonomy. The relationship both secured me and gave me freedom.

Are you aware of an area in your life that has been secured by training wheels that no longer serves you, perhaps a way of thinking or being? Take a few moments to reflect on that now.

In chapter two we used the questions from Byron Katie's The Work to guide our reflection: (1) Is it true? (2) Can you absolutely know that it is true? (3) How do you react, what happens, when you believe that thought? (4) Who or what would you be without that thought? How do these questions lead you to purgation or freedom?

Reflect on how you have sensed God moving you from a system of belief into one of belonging, a relational way of being that transcends your belief system that has gotten in the way, like my rules-based belief system.

4

PERFECTIONISM AND
THE GOOD GIRL

J'm the kind of person who likes to study personality types. I have studied those discussed in Florence Littauer's book *Personality Plus* and have taken the DISC personality profile along with numerous other tests, for reasons that all boil down to trying to figure out what in the heck I am here for, who I really am, what's not me, and what's just debris picked up along the way. Of all the personality profiles out there, the one I like the most is the Enneagram, which assigns a number to the various personality types. The Enneagram shows how each of us reflects an aspect of God's character. Our challenge is to show the image of God without our dark side, our ego side, taking over.

According to the Enneagram's nine type descriptions, I am a One—the perfectionist, who drives myself crazy with my own expectations of how I think life and things should be. In *The*

Enneagram Made Easy, authors Renee Baron and Elizabeth Wagele write that Ones "are motivated by the need to live life the right way, including improving themselves and the world around them." I'm a performance addict trying to emulate the perfect image of God, but a bunch of crap gets in the way—stuff like judgmentalism, self-righteousness, intolerance, and inflexibility. This has often left me disappointed with myself and others, burdened from taking on too much responsibility, and devaluing my worth and my productivity, leading to lots of tension and anxiety for myself and, unfortunately, for those around me as well.

My cousin Ricky once told me, "You were so bossy when we were kids." He was absolutely right about that. I apologized and asked him to forgive me and said I was just a kid. But at our worst, Ones are bossy and think we alone are capable of getting this whole thing worked out to the glory of God, hallelujah, *amen!* The rest of y'all are just messing around. Don't you know that Jesus is coming? You better not just look busy; you better *be* busy about his kingdom or you are never going to see the gates of heaven. You know that, right?

Sigh. Yeah, I'm a One. God, help me, please!

Striving for Acceptance

According to the Enneagram, Ones strive for the ideal—the operative word being *strive*. We strive to be the best. In *Personality Types: Using the Enneagram for Self-Discovery,* authors Don Richard Riso and Russ Hudson write:

> To this personality type, the advice of "Desiderata" sounds foolish and dangerous: "Beyond a wholesome discipline,

be gentle with yourself. You are a child of the universe, no less than the trees and the stars; you have a right to be here. And whether or not it is clear to you, no doubt the universe is unfolding as it should."

The words of the Desiderata have been a great comfort to me because they remind me that God is at work here in the aftermath of my crash and that I belong without any effort on my part. For too long I felt that I had to earn my birthright, and my lingering anxiety was calmed by knowing I have a right to be here because God has deemed it so. When I read this on the recovery journey, I was grateful for a clear word reminding me that I could let go of doubt and that God would remain present and would orchestrate life for me even as much as God was creating trees and stars and sustaining the universe. I needed this reassurance. In the midst of feeling unsure of where the depression and its dark night were leading me, these words gave me hope. One positive quality of Ones is that we value learning and finding insight into our lives, and that is serving me well even now.

We Ones are not gentle with ourselves. I can be downright abusive to myself, which negatively affects those around me. These days I have a tangible indicator of the need to be gentle with myself. Meditation has been a gift in allowing me to become present to what had been unconscious actions and thought patterns. I have noticed that when I meditate and my mind wanders, as it does quite frequently, if I yell at myself and say something like, *Get back over here, we are meditating for God's sake!*, my body responds with a medieval hot flash. All I think about in those moments is stripping off my clothes—my skin if

I could—and leaping head first into a pool of ice-cold water, like in the old-school "Nestea Plunge" commercials. Just typing those words caused my body to respond with a flash of hormone-generated heat. Lord, have mercy.

How wise are these words of the Desiderata: "Beyond a wholesome discipline." Yet the challenge for me is knowing what "wholesome discipline" is. Discipline is the tool I have always used to program myself into submission to maintain my good girl image, avoid punishment/hell, and earn my right to be, let alone to be *here*. For so long I have felt that I had to earn my right to be *me*, to be *here*. Somewhere deeply imbedded in my psyche I have been striving to be accepted and wanted in just the right way.

This comes through in my earliest school photos. You can see little Juanita striving to look and be picture-perfect: every hair in place, blouse collars pointing due south just as they should. In my eyes you can see the makings of a type A personality—the kind of little girl who learns to cook early so she can be a mother's helper, someone responsible and eager to take on adult tasks, someone serious and hardworking. My maternal grandmother, Madear, noted that I was a fast learner. My cousins would add, "And a know-it-all" who tried to keep them all in line. The discipline I received as a child seemed harsh to me, so I made it my business to avoid the need for other people's correction by simply controlling myself—and I tried to help others do the same. I was a child thinking like a child (see 1 Corinthians 13:11). The problem is that I carried this thinking into adulthood. I had made my life about pleasing people and avoiding punishment like a good child, but that was no longer serving me. The crash was the beginning of putting away childish things.

I was angry that no one was validating my worth despite all of my hard work, striving, and effort. With the onset of the crash, my life seemed to be unraveling on all sides. But in that place, frazzled, void of emotion, and numb as I was, I sensed something stirring for my greater good, and that was where I found solace. The light hadn't pierced the darkness yet, but hope was out there. I knew it. Hope not as a feeling—I was too numb for that—but hope as an ideal, like a type of dream that seemed possible even then.

Like all Enneagram numbers, Ones have their negative aspects or the places where some healing could go a long way, but there are also some light and positive aspects of being a One. I am working to be present and aware of those as much as the negative aspects. In *The Enneagram Made Easy* the authors suggest that Ones at their best are enthusiastic, self-accepting, and more spontaneous. We look for the good in situations, we make plans to enjoy things just for fun, we get in touch with deeper feelings, and we become involved in creativity and find ways to be engaged in the arts. Healthy Ones learn to relax and simply enjoy life, valuing themselves and taking a lighter approach to how they see life and the world. Ones can be interesting, inspiring, self-disciplined, reasonable, responsible, and dedicated; they operate with a moral compass and practice what they preach, and are often seen as efficient, hardworking, and dependable. Until this season of the crash, I hadn't made time and space to open myself to what the Enneagram had to teach me. Yep, there was some unfolding happening here, and I was grateful for the reality of knowing that it was happening in me even as a One. This unfolding offered me a different way of seeing how I could be and who I could be and gave me a way to dream again.

PAUSE TO REFLECT

What personality trait has caused you the most concern? How has it ruled your life?

If you are not familiar with the Enneagram, you might consider exploring it via the Enneagram Institute website (enneagram institute.com) or a book such as *The Enneagram Made Easy* or *The Road Back to You.*

Interlude

A FAMILY'S DILEMMA—
REFLECTIONS OF RYAN AND RUDY

*I*n the midst of the crash I was in bed for eighteen to twenty hours a day. At one point the ringtone on my phone started to leave me feeling panicked and anxious and physically gasping for breath like an emphysema patient, although I have never smoked. It became clear that anxiety had become a companion to the depression I was living with, and my psychiatrist added it to my diagnosis.

Rudy suggested that I turn off the phone ringer. I limited my phone calls to speaking to my husband at noon each day when he'd call to check on me. Without the daily, loving support of my family and the encouragement of the St. John's family I don't know how I would have maintained hope for recovery.

I asked my daughters, Morgan and Ryan, and husband, Rudy, to share their reflections about what it was like for them. Morgan was diagnosed in college with attention deficit disorder. With a bit of wit and a big smile she said, "Mommy, I remember very little from that time; perhaps the ADD served me well for once."

Ryan

I don't think I really realized what was going on at first. I thought my mom was just sick and needed rest. I recall thinking after a few days passed that something more was happening, and feeling fearful and sad that she wasn't able to interact with us and be present as she had been before. But I knew she'd get better at some point and things would go back to "normal."

After some time passed and my mommy was being treated for depression, I felt simultaneously protective of her as she recovered—not wanting anything to happen that would send her back to bed—and also ashamed. Despite having had some knowledge about mental health challenges through seeing people at church and feeling that our family was a safe space to talk about things, it felt different knowing that *my* mom was dealing with depression.

I didn't feel ashamed of my mom. I mostly felt like I didn't want people to know. Maybe I didn't want their questions—which was the opposite of how we managed things. The openness and this new level of vulnerability took some getting used to. I recall people asking about her every week at church. I didn't really know what to tell them and felt frustrated and angry that they would ask her daughter (mature for my age but a child nonetheless) about her and why she wasn't there. It was intrusive and lacked understanding and empathy. Thankfully I didn't learn until later that people were commenting on the state of her marriage to my dad. Had I known that back then it would have been too much to deal with.

It took lots of reflection for me to recall these feelings and memories. I think this is in part related to my own emotional state at the time. I was on the verge of my own depressive episode and probably also dealing with trauma-related symptoms.

One thing that stands out to me was the conversation my mom had with Morgan and me later in her recovery about her changing duties at church. Being at church almost seven days a week was literally all I had known, and I was unsure and afraid of what our lives would be like if she was home more; the idea seemed foreign to me. I remember later reflecting on how happy I was that she made that change and how I wished it had happened sooner. Slowing down our family pace and being more present to one another was a welcome change.

Rudy

From the moment it was clear that we would no longer experience Juanita in the way we had grown accustomed to experiencing her, especially her laughter and smile, fear, anxiety, and adrenalin kicked in for me. The fear I experienced was a byproduct of my insecurity as I filled in Juanita's place with our daughters in the rituals she had established with them during their early childhood with her. Rituals like combing their hair and putting it into styles commonly worn by preteenagers. One of my daughters reminded me of my using office-supply rubber bands to keep their hair presentable. I didn't realize that those little black rubber bands their mom had always used were unique.

Every morning after the crash, we would go through a modified ritual, now with me instead of their mom, who struggled to get out of bed every day for months. I also experienced anxiety as a result of feelings of inadequacy about my ability to provide the nurture that came so easily to Juanita. Both girls were in the throes of difficult middle-school experiences, which meant having a broad range of emotional responses every day. The emotional swings, combined with their mother's inability to be present to them, enhanced the intensity of every crisis.

Eventually my adrenalin reached a constant level of ten. The girls often remind me of how I drove off on numerous occasions while they were still getting in the car and a few times while they were literally hanging on to the door as I pressed the gas pedal. Today, they still shout, "Not in yet!" to ensure I don't replay their childhood nightmare of clinging to the car door.

In spite of that season being one of the most challenging moments of our thirty-four years together, and even though it was a daily struggle to find our way through Juanita's bout with depression, I am reminded of how strong the lifelong bond of love became with me and my daughters. Hopefully they were reassured that they had two parents who loved them dearly.

5

COULD I JUST HIT BOTTOM ALREADY?

nother morning dawned with me lying across my bed, lethargic, tired to the bone. Weeks into the depression, my body seemed to weigh hundreds of pounds more than my 5′4″ frame could support. Yet the weight was emotional, not physical: the weight of wrong thinking, delusion, disappointment, despair, grief, and sheer soul exhaustion. The kind of weight felt when hopelessness drops its tonnage on us, similar to when the cartoon character Wile E. Coyote is running for dear life and a boulder suddenly falls from the sky and lands on him. Splat.

I had come to the end of myself. Couldn't do a thing. Nada. I needed to go to the restroom, but I didn't have the foggiest idea how to get out of the bed. The mild sense of dread I felt turned into full-blown panic. I felt powerless, frazzled, as though my

brain was scrambling with sirens going off in my head: "Red
Alert! She can't get out of bed!" I thought, *Let's try to think
through this. Perhaps I could roll out of bed onto the floor.*

At that moment, I heard God say, "Look at you. You can't do
anything for me. But I love you." But what I internalized as I lay
there, unable to get out of the bed, was "Look at you. You're
worthless. You have no capacity to be used by me now. I can't
rely on you at all. You've blown it now. Well, I still pity you
enough to love you, considering."

This was the God I thought I had found—the God of my
childhood—showing up just the way so many had described
God to be: a harsh, punitive taskmaster. This was my understanding of who God was, and it shaped how I had been living.
My life was a narrative of avoiding punishment for all my sin,
and now, apparently, I had blown it, and this was my punishment.

Thankfully, my temporary paralysis forced me to stay there
long enough for God to clarify that what I had internalized and
what God had said were two totally different notions. God
spoke again, this time with an explanation: "Look at you. You
have totally worn yourself out seeking everybody's approval,
striving for perfection, making sure you are perceived as pro-
ductive. But you can't do anything to earn my love. Don't you
know that I love you—period, totally, without any action on
your part? Juanita, you don't have to work to earn my love. It
pleases me to give it to you freely."

I felt the warmth of tears pooling in the corners of my eyes,
tears out of a very deep place in my soul. And at that moment,
I felt loved and understood even as I realized that I had God all
wrong. God was not Judge Judy or a divine Santa Claus trying
to catch me being naughty. God was *not* asking me to prove

myself worthy. I had used up so much of my life energy driven by the weight of that belief that it was no wonder I had exhausted myself. I could see that now.

A sense of relief flooded me—mind, body, and spirit. I felt so relieved from the weight of a lifetime of unmet expectations that I had neatly arranged in compressed packing cubes. In my mind if you're gonna carry emotional baggage, it should be neatly presented and compressed for maximum hauling. I had never imagined that my beliefs could weigh my life down that way. At that moment it was as though I had been given wings and had become weightless. It was freedom I had never felt before. *Light* and *airy* only partially describe how I felt; perhaps *magical* is a good start.

Descending into the Darkness

Despite my newfound freedom from the crushing weight of expectations I had been living under, I found myself descending deeper and deeper into a dark pit. If I was wrong about what it meant to be loved by God, did that mean there were other things I had gotten wrong regarding God? When I slept I had a falling sensation, and as I fell I hoped to find something in the darkness that I could grab hold of. I wanted the perpetual falling to cease. Only later did it occur to me that my sense of falling was symbolic and that it would enable me to grow from a place of depth.

Thankfully, by eventually hitting rock bottom I came to know the God who had found me. This was not the god of my childhood making. This God was present to me in fullness during the falling, present just like my daddy had been when the training wheels had been taken off of my pink bike. I had to fall past the depth of my willpower to stop believing that I was strong enough to pull myself out. I had to fall past the depth of my knowledge to stop believing that my intellect would get me through this. I had to fall past the depth of my determination and even my physical stamina to a place where only God could provide security. I had to, as Saint John of the Cross wrote, be purged of all my attachments to who I had believed myself to be and who I had believed God to be. I came to see that this whole process was more than a physical and mental diagnosis by my psychiatrist; this was about helping me build a life I wanted to live, a life present to a God who desired that I would live fully into love.

At the bottom I settled into the kindness and incredible peace of God, the kind of peace I've heard spoken of by those who have experienced a near-death episode. There, I was surrounded by love I had never before experienced, love that was dense and filled the space all around me. This love stayed with me from that point on in the bottom of the dark pit, accompanying me just as consistently as my cat Angel had been doing, lying on my bed with me during the crash. Here, in this place, there was no fear, no anxiety, just pure love. Here even the darkness was a kind of light generated by the constant exposure to the presence of God.

The experience brought to mind John 14:3: "I go and prepare a place for you . . . so that where I am, there you may be also" (NRSV). When I hit bottom, dread left me and the darkness became light, so my whole being was illuminated. The love I felt silenced my anxiety. There at the bottom of the well it was as though God had been waiting for me and had prepared a feast for me—food like peace, stillness, compassion, and kindness—that fed the deepest part of my starved soul.

Howard Thurman, African American theologian, mystic, and dean emeritus of Marsh Chapel, Boston University, wrote in his book *The Creative Encounter,*

> Religious experience in its profoundest dimensions is the finding of man by God and the finding of God by man.... It is in his religious experience that he sees himself from another point of view. In a very real sense he is stripped of everything and he stands with no possible protection.... The new center is found, and it is often like giving birth to a new self.

At the bottom of the well I had been found by God and I had found God, and indeed I had found a new center, a place of communion with the Creator.

PAUSE TO REFLECT

Have you had an experience that caused you to feel as though you too had come to the end of yourself? Where your experiences of yourself no longer satisfied you or sustained you? Reflect on that time.

How have you encountered the reality of God so far? What has been your experience with darkness? Have you had a sense of falling away from all you had known of God only to have God show up in ways or in a place that you didn't expect?

6

FINDING MY BEING

I have often heard people in recovery talk about hitting rock bottom. Hitting my own bottom of depression has enabled me to come to an amazing awareness: I had been sourcing my life from an illusion. I had been running on empty for a long time. Not until I hit rock bottom did I realize that the gas gauge within me was damaged. I needed a deeper reality. I was beginning to know the meaning of Acts 17:28: "In him we live and move and have our being."

The Source of My Being

My being is the me that manifested in divine love at my conception. In Christ there is fullness of life, not the coma that I had lived through rote activity and damning rules. I had lived as though my activities sourced my life—as though they gave me life—only to find that while they may have seemed like good activities, in time they literally drained the life out of me. I needed to be recharged, but I didn't know this until I was on empty; hitting the bottom helped me to know what my empty was like.

Some folks have a longer battery life than others. Perhaps their lives are not so demanding. Perhaps some of us are poorly charged for the tasks of life awaiting us. Or we start out of the gate at such a pace that by our mid-thirties we find ourselves depleted. For all my life to this point I had presumed that *my* effort sustained me, crazy as it sounds. But through the depression, I was being freed from those notions of self-sustainability. Thank God for this awakening. In the depth of the darkness I found my being in the presence of God. I knew intuitively that all I was had been in God alone. It was clear that in the same way the lotus flower blooms in muddy waters, God brought me to life amid the muddiness of my rules, perfectionism, and striving. There was nothing in that awareness but pure gratitude, relief really. Now I knew where my sustenance was coming from, and I was being fueled and filled.

I had been parched by life, sucked dry. I was humbled, grateful beyond words, thrilled speechless in the presence of God who was quenching in me a thirst that only God could satisfy. I was being energized and charged to live and move and to know what it meant to be fully alive. God met me at the level of my thirst. There was no effort on my part, no scheduling, no doing, no talking, just being, and being fully aware that that was all I needed. My aliveness was God's doing, and being was my response.

God's Crash School

As I gained consciousness after the initial months of the crash, I became increasingly aware that I was in a school of sorts; I was being homeschooled by God. God was instructing me on how to live out of my ground of being, and God was that ground. I was learning to be still, to be calm, to be cared for, and to know God's love. I was being taught that to live my life in the presence of God was to know total sufficiency. I was learning how to be present to God's unconditional and limitless love, and I was growing to see that love wasn't outside of me but rather in my own heart. I was experiencing it as power flowing through me, and it was giving me life. God was instructing me to stop *doing* and just *be*. I was being invited to surrender. In the Twelve Step program they call this turning your life over to the care of God.

"You are experiencing a dark night of the soul," my friend Marie Noack said on one of our phone calls. Marie and I had become sister friends after meeting at a Renovaré Spiritual Formation event. We were both young mothers, and our hearts connected; meeting her was like finding a soul sister, one who spoke my language and shared my growing delight in experiencing God in new ways beyond my limited set of spiritual practices. She became a teacher for me, a real companion on the way. We often called each other simultaneously, so the phone wouldn't even ring, yet we were on the line each having just thought of the other. We had this happen so often that we laughed with great joy, thanking God for this beautiful bond.

When Marie named my depression and the journey I was on as a dark night of the soul, it all made sense. This was not just about a crashing collapse of a life that needed to be rebuilt but about getting a new life altogether—a beautiful, God-infused, God-constructed life.

I love those remodeling shows on cable TV where the stars of the show remodel someone's home and the homeowners are delighted with the results even after finding out there were serious air conditioning problems or code violations that had to be corrected. The homeowners are pleased with their remodeled, like-new home.

The dark night of the soul is no simple remodel of the soul, the self that I had grown accustomed to; no, this is deconstruction down to the foundation. God takes the suffering that had brought me to the dark pit and transforms it by freeing me of addictions, resentments, codependency, and attachments to ways of being that I believed were the essence of my life. The dark night of the soul is the awareness that I am moving out of a place of disorientation—the crash—into a new truth, a new orientation, where the reality of God is revealed in transformative ways. All that had brought consolation no longer serves to support my life. The dark night is the beginning of a new day and a new way of living; it's the realization that my life had been solely what my ego had made it to be, in my mind. Here in this dark night I was being invited into a new way of *being*—in the world, with myself, and with God. Had I been a caterpillar, the dark night would have been my lonesome experience of transformation in the chrysalis. Only time would tell if the emerging transformation would yield new life as a butterfly.

Discovering New Spiritual Practices

A year or so before the crash, I had been introduced to Richard Foster, author of *Celebration of Discipline*. His book was on my bookshelf, but I had only glanced at it occasionally. Meeting Richard and learning of his ministry Renovaré exposed me to spiritual practices that I wasn't aware of and introduced me to scholars and authors like Dallas Willard, Emilie Griffin, James Bryan Smith, Glandion Carney, and, later, Chris Hall and other spiritual icons of our century. I was invited to serve on Richard's ministry team and found myself frequently sitting with people I had grown to admire and revere. I often asked myself, *How did I get here? How did I get to sit with these incredible spiritual gurus and mystics?* In their presence I felt like a kid getting to have lunch at school with my heroes and sheroes. They were so humble, and they made it so easy to be present, but that didn't stop me from wondering just how the gods had seen fit to invite me into this orbit.

One spiritual practice I became acquainted with was lectio divina—praying with the Scriptures. I was first introduced to this practice in a small group with Marie Noack when I attended her weekly centering prayer gathering a few months before the crash. Later, months into my recovery, I experienced lectio divina at the Cenacle Retreat House in Houston, where I qualified as a certified spiritual director, trained to companion others on their spiritual journey under Sister Mary Dennison, the program's founder. I had been interested in the Cenacle's training, but the timing never seemed right. Now, as I was rebuilding my life, I had plenty of time. So, I applied and was accepted into the program about two years after the crash. Lectio was a common practice in the training program, and I grew to love it and share it whenever I had the opportunity, especially with my children.

Lectio divina invites slow, meditative reading of a few verses at a time so we chew them like a cow chews its cud. Cows have digestive chambers through which food is moved back and forth until all that is life-giving has been digested. The act of chewing and regurgitating is where the word *meditation* comes from. Though I studied about twenty hours a week to prepare for Bible study or to preach, I lacked the discipline of reading my Bible so it could read me. Through lectio divina then and now I learn more about myself, God, God's love for me, and who I am in God. God's presence in the text gives me life. Sometimes it offers clarity to my thinking or invites me to reflect on what I had imposed on the text, often to find new meaning and insight. Let me explain what I mean. I enjoy when Mommie cooks her Thanksgiving meal. I always ask for extra dressing since hers is the best. I love the savory spices she uses and the way her cornbread dressing awakens good memories in me while it bakes in the oven—memories of being loved by her. The smell of Thanksgiving dinner fills the house. I don't know her recipe—I've never asked; I simply receive it as a gift, a token of her affection and care toward me. Now, my father's eggnog isn't made from scratch, but I can sense the love with which he offers it. Growing up, Daddy would have Nat King Cole singing "The Christmas Song" on the stereo. He would pull out the special-occasion glasses with the silver band around the top. Nothing says the holidays like the ambiance Daddy creates when offering his flavorful and fragrant eggnog.

That's what lectio divina is like. It's not just a meal, but a meal with love and memories. We walk away awakened to something deeper and more life-giving than just knowing about the text—we come to know the Beloved of our soul and the care that went into providing this gift of soul food.

As I enter into a lectio divina reading, I am aware that something in me will have the opportunity to be more gently grounded in God's love and presence. Something will be offered that will robustly invigorate me or will offer a new awareness or hope concerning circumstances that are not life-giving for me.

Will You Let Me Take Care of You?

I love Psalm 23. Madear, my maternal grandmother, taught it to me before I could read, and in lectio divina I came to see for the first time how the Shepherd cares for me and has invited me to allow that care in my life.

After meditating on the text during one of my frequent visits to the Cenacle for my classes in spiritual direction, I created a simple, childlike piece of art that sits on my desk and reminds me of the experience. It was then the Spirit asked, "Will you let me care for you?"

Tears stirred behind my eyelids, and I exhaled deeply. God had been longing to care for me, but I had been too busy to receive it. For so long I hadn't wanted to bother God, I hadn't wanted to seem, well, needy. God watched me do my thing while waiting patiently for me to slow down enough to desire God's guidance, healing, love, and companionship.

Lectio divina invites us to come home to God in a childlike way—full of trust—that encourages us to lay aside everything else. We are invited to lay aside masks, projections, fears, hurts. Here in God's presence, in this place of being, there is spaciousness, luminosity, and an awareness of being deeply loved.

PAUSE TO REFLECT

To practice lectio divina, select a passage of Scripture or other sacred reading. You can use Psalm 23 or another passage of choice. Use only five to seven verses to focus on at any one sitting. Have a pad and pen with you to make notes.

Take a moment and breathe. When inhaling, be aware of the cool air coming into your nostrils, and likewise the warm air that exits them when exhaling. Just be with your breath. Do this for a couple of minutes. This is the first step for preparing to be present to lectio divina, making conscious contact with God as the breath of life present in your awareness.

SILENCIO. Quiet yourself and offer yourself to God. I find the breathing helps with this.

LECTIO. Read your passage slowly out loud and listen to what is being read. Listen as though God is speaking to you. Notice what word or phrase seems to catch your attention. Sit with that word or phrase and marinate in it as a gift from God to you.

MEDITATIO. Read the passage aloud a second time. How is your word or phrase speaking into your current life? Reflect. Here is the experience of the cow chewing its cud that I mentioned earlier. Allow yourself to enter into the scene of the reading using your imagination. What are you hearing, seeing, smelling in the scene? Observe with the curiosity of a child.

ORATIO. Read the passage aloud a third time. Respond. How might God be speaking to you from this reading? This is the space to ask God, "What are you saying to me?" This is the space of conversation with God, the space of prayer. Stay open to insight—how are you being offered guidance or new awareness? How might you respond to God's invitation flowing out of your dialogue together? Know God's love in this space. Feel free to jot down your thoughts.

CONTEMPLATIO. Contemplatio is the deep marinating, sitting with what you have heard and felt. Stay here; linger in your experience. Rest. Breathe in deeply and slowly, exhale deeply and fully. Capture what you have known here and carry it throughout your day. Bring it back to mind as you move through your day. Stay in this space with God for as long as you feel it is good and right for you.

ACTIO. How has your experience invited you to be present to yourself or to be present to others? What action, if any, are you invited into out of this space of being with God?

Interlude

DOING . . . DOING . . . DONE!

The Proverbs 31 woman messed me up.

I can't say for how long the model woman, as she is sometimes called, or as King Jimmy (my nickname for the King James Version of the Bible) calls her, the "virtuous woman" (v. 10), had been my ideal, my "shero," a go-to woman of virtue and holiness. I had made the habit of praying for Rudy in Psalm 1:1-3 when we first married. I was so grateful that in the early days of our marriage a wise older woman told me that it would be important to pray a Scripture over my husband's life, and Psalm 1 seemed appropriate. Call it the Spirit leading me. I would read the passage, and then everywhere I could I'd insert Rudy's name: "Blessed is Rudy who walks not in the council of the ungodly. . . ." I have prayed that way daily for years now, and it has been amazing and profound to see how that passage has shaped Rudy's life. One day I decided, heck, if he needed prayer and a Scripture, perhaps I needed one as well! I had always been drawn to the woman described in Proverbs 31, so I began to pray for myself that I would be this virtuous woman in the life of my family and in my circles of influence.

This model woman seemed to embody everything that I thought I wanted in life: She is recognized for her industry. She is valued. Her children see her as happy. And her husband praises her and trusts in her abilities, honors her, and rewards her by giving her a share in the fruit of her hands, which in her time was uncommon culturally. She was ideal. I mean, come on, she managed her home well, got up early, and provided food for her household and servant girls. I knew I was short on servant girls until a women's conference speaker named the washing machine and the clothes dryer as "servant girls" along with the servant-girl dishwasher and the servant-girl microwave. Yet all she did was piss me off when I was already overwhelmed and suffocated by the demands on my life, time, and sanity. Then I began to feel guilty for not being grateful for my mechanized servant girls while life exacted a toll on my mind, body, and spirit. In the days leading up to the crash I could totally relate to the iconic scene I had watched years earlier in the *I Love Lucy* episode "Job Switching," where Lucy and Ethel worked on the chocolate candy conveyor belt. When Lucy couldn't keep up but lied and pretended she could, the supervisor applauded her tenacity and increased the belt speed, completely overwhelming Lucy and Ethel, which led to their termination.

Before the crash, I didn't realize I was lying to myself when people would casually ask me how I was and I would respond with a well-chiseled smile and say, "Fine!" I was in such denial about my ability to keep up. I didn't know to say, "*Help!* I need help!" The Proverbs woman became an icon I felt tormented by. She was my version of the belt speed being increased. Lucy and Ethel were terminated, removed from the candy conveyor belt, and saved from their lies.

In so many ways I have come to appreciate and even be grateful that my mind and body did for me what I could not do for myself: they shut down and took me off my conveyor belt. No dramatic scenes, no "crazy" acting in public, just a phone call on August 27 to babble that I wasn't coming back.

7

GETTING FREE OF MY NOTIONS

*F*or much of my life I was consumed by childhood notions of what it meant to be a good wife, a good mother,
and a good pastor. The ideal of being *good* pervaded my world;
it was my way of constructing meaning, purpose, and identity.

I completely related to Jesus' words in Luke 9:25, when he
asked, "What good is it for someone to gain the whole world,
and yet lose or forfeit their very self?" Before the crash, I lived
for accomplishment and the approval of the various authority
figures in my life, all who happened to be male. They were
simply the earthly image of the God whose approval I wanted
and who would undoubtedly reward me and free me from
eternal punishment.

Day by day, I boxed myself in with these notions; mine had
become a tight, rigid, little life. There were times of laughter but
little joy. I've heard it said that you can't mix what you can't
measure. That seems to apply to my life. I had no means for
calculating joy and assumed that being an optimist was sufficient.

I was happy with my marriage—Rudy and I are a real team. We knew how to divide the workload at church and at home. Our home was peaceful in a chaotic sort of way. I mean, there was always laundry to do, meals to forage, and homework and school projects, but I wanted our home to be filled with love and peace, and I worked at it as best I knew how.

Learning from a Dream

As I was learning more about my good-girl notions, I awakened one particular morning from a crazy-ass dream. In the dream I had just gotten back to town, and apparently Rudy had asked me to join him at a restaurant. But he had not mentioned that we would have guests accompanying us. I get there and am overwhelmed because too many others are present. One young woman in particular seemed to need way too much of Pastor Rudy's attention, and I became frustrated, jealous, and bitter. When I awakened and realized that it was only a dream, I quickly went into deny-the-feelings mode. But this time I caught myself and said, *Wait, the dream may not be real, but the feelings are alive and kicking!* I decided right then and there to allow myself to be present to the feelings of jealousy and bitterness.

It was eye opening to see how often I routinely flushed my feelings away to seek a more good-girl feeling. I showered and headed to Mass. I wrestled with holding on to the feelings. Ideally, if I am gonna wrestle, why not do it in the presence of God? God alone can referee and determine the winner. Plus, for me to settle the matter that quickly would only mean that I had resorted to my old ways, habits of disassociation, and ignoring my feelings.

I was on a retreat that day at Lebh Shomea, a retreat center in south Texas, and was still processing the dream when the morning mass began. Before I knew it, the time had come to share with our neighbor what we had heard that stood out for us during the readings. I had nothing to say; I couldn't even remember the readings. Sister Marie, the hermit at Lebh Shomea, went first, thank God; I hoped maybe something would come to me while she shared. It did not. So I said, "I was distracted. I had a dream, and I was left with feelings of jealousy and bitterness, so I couldn't even hear the readings this morning." Sister Marie responded that "sometimes when we have such strong feelings in a dream it means that God is at work healing them." Father Kelly returned to the podium and gave the homily. I don't recall what he said, but I began to cry, tears welling up and flowing down my face.

Then I heard these words as Father Kelly looked directly at me: *Todo pasa solo Dios basta.* "Everything passes; only God remains." He said our concepts pass, our ideals pass, our feelings pass, and only God remains. I whispered, "Thank you, God."

Sometimes I forget that I am fully human, but I am. I have feelings of inadequacy and jealousy and bitterness that I would rather not see, feel, or admit. Can't we all just be mad, happy, sad, or glad? And if we are mad, can't we just decide to be glad instead? It's amazing how our limited childhood programs for happiness, the individual beliefs we each form in childhood about what leads to happiness, can wreak havoc on our hearts and minds, even once the light of the truth has been shined on them.

I once heard Father Richard Rohr say, on a livestream from his Center for Action and Contemplation, "We all play out our childhood programs for happiness, and as adults that can become our hell." When we do the work of putting away our childish things, "our childhood program for happiness" can become the new realities that transform us. The work is to move beyond our limited systems of belief and belonging and into the experience of knowing God.

I am fully human, and that means I am created in the image of God. If, as the Old Testament says, God is a jealous God, then his daughter can carry his traits, right? The good news for me is that I get to talk to God about letting go of these old ways of being, these feelings that do not give life. If I am jealous, then I can decide how much energy I want to put into jealousy or shift into something more life-giving. Jealousy is about envy and resentment, suspicion, judgment, and distrust. If I can remember that I am the one with those feelings and that I am the one who can change my mind about carrying those feelings and the story I have constructed that has allowed these feelings to emerge, then I can begin to heal. Those feelings are the feelings of childhood; they are not new, although they do raise their ugly heads. These are not feelings generated by my dream or by the imaginary woman in the dream, but rather the dream was a vehicle that enabled me to see myself more clearly.

I believe psychologist Carl Jung would say that the Dream Maker needed me to pay attention to what I had allowed to go unchecked in my thinking. It was revealed so I could acknowledge it, embrace it, and let it go. It is revealed to be healed. That is my childhood story of pain. I can choose to think new thoughts and create a new life-giving story for myself.

Everything passes; *only God remains.* Thank you, Jesus. I do not have to keep living this as my reality. I can choose to let it go!

First Corinthians 13:11 says, "When I was a child, I spoke like a child, I thought like a child, I reasoned like a child; when I became an adult, I put an end to childish ways" (NRSV).

Wouldn't it be great if as children we had a ritual for putting away all the beliefs and notions that would no longer serve us as adults? But then I guess that's what our suffering is really about—helping us to grow up and away from our limiting beliefs into the only thing that remains, relationship with God.

Thank You, Oprah!

One day I decided to watch the *Oprah* show. Oprah asked a question of her guest that I have heard her ask her guests before: "What do you know for sure?" His response drew me in: "What I know for sure is that I am." He began to expound on the "I am" as being made known or revealed out of the stillness, out of silence. He said that the soul has nothing to achieve, nothing to prove to anyone. As he spoke, I heard that I was more than my personality quizzes, more than my memories, more than my emotional and physical pain, more than my skin color, hair texture, preferred snack food, or the neighborhood I grew up in. None of those really spoke to the essence of who I was.

I could sense that when the Spirit first asked me, "Who are you?" I have always believed that when the student is ready, the teacher will appear. I listened, and my soul leaned in. In my head I could almost hear my girlfriend's voice saying, "Girl, are you listening to this? Good. Take notes!"

Listening to Oprah's guest reminded me of a teaching Rudy and I had experienced while on a couples retreat with Joe and Yolande Herron-Palmore, associate pastors at Windsor Village United Methodist Church at the time. The Palmores used the psychological tool called Johari's Window as a way of revealing to us that there is more than one image being projected of the self. In this exercise a four-pane window is used to illustrate that there are four components to an individual: the me I see, the me I don't want you to see, the me you see but I don't (commonly called the shadow self), and the me God alone sees. All of the panes contribute to the "I am." Aspects of our selves are hidden from our view, but the good news is that all of who I am is known by God, even if much of it is still a mystery to me. This exercise resonated strongly with me. For example, most people don't know that I am introverted, but it is a part of who I am. Until the crash I had no idea that I didn't get my energy from being in the mix with people but rather that I need silence and solitude so I can have the energy, the capacity, to be present with others.

The reality is that we all show up in a couple of different versions of our selves. One form I'll call the façade version of Juanita, that is, the performance identity. Until the crash I believed this to be the real me. This is Juanita facing frustration; operating out of ego, vulnerability, fear, joy, moments of fleeting peace, the ebb and flow of pleasure, accomplishment and failure; longing for life to be fair or kind; hoping for freedom, that her roles would offer validation and her improvements would allow her to finally measure up—the version that I had believed to be the real me. This is a good enough version—a way of seeing oneself. The apostle Paul, however, called this version of self "the flesh" (Romans 7:5 NKJV).

The second version of self flows out of a deeper dimension, the *me* named the soul, the timeless essence of me, my being. This is the fundamental me, the me I am coming to know in stillness and silence, the ultimate self, the me who senses without resorting to judgment just so I can feel good about myself. Jesus called this my everlasting life, so I knew what the Palmores meant when they talked about the me that only God sees.

The crash left my performance identity bankrupt. I felt hollow and lifeless. The part of me that judged was the first fallout from the crash. But I often sensed this judging presence lurking around, waiting to attack me for being weak and vulnerable. It felt like someone whispering in tones of condemnation, "If only you had just tried harder."

While I was grateful for the psychiatrist, talk therapy with my therapist, and medication, still more was needed. Oprah's guest gave me hope that there was more to me than my performance identity—which had been a heavy cross to bear. The guest's timely comment on the deeper dimension helped make sense of my incessant awareness of falling. I have often heard the spiritual journey described as ascending—journeying upward—but a deeper dimension can only be achieved if one has descended. In Alcoholics Anonymous this is called hitting rock bottom. I made a note in my journal as I was reflecting on the bottom business once my eyes were open to the gift that it had come to be.

God, I am so reminded that you had been whispering "Be still" in my ears for so long prior to this crash. So, this is what you meant. I never would have imagined this, never did in fact, that you meant really still, deep down in a John 15 abiding kind of way. Dang. Wish I had asked you how to get here instead of assuming that I knew what you meant. Not only is there a spaciousness here, there is so much silence, but not a scary kind like right before something crazy happens in a thriller movie. This is a kind of silence that you can feel; there's quiet calm and peace here. Here I am in the presence of divine love. This is so much more than I could have ever imagined. If this is rock bottom, then I'm grateful. I know now that in the stillness not only do I get to know something more of God, but I get to know something more of the me that God knows, just like the Palmores had taught us. Here I know what it is to be known and loved, having nothing to prove to anyone. In this space I am valued, and I know total acceptance and overwhelming freedom in simply just being.

PAUSE TO REFLECT

My crash has made me aware of many nuances in my daily existence. Stress can literally take one's breath away. When oxygen isn't flowing to the brain, we minimize the capacity to dream or imagine any new possibilities at all. I realized that I had made a habit of holding my breath throughout the day. I had so much coming at me prior to the crash that I was holding my breath, waiting on the next shoe to drop. Flight attendants have for years advised us to put our oxygen mask on first before assisting someone else with theirs. I have found that when all else is failing, I can stop, drop, and breathe!

Breathe in deeply and exhale deeply and slowly. While there are hundreds of thousands of ways of breathing, the technique that works best is the one you are attentive to. The bottom line is, be intentionally present to your breath. If smokers can take time to smoke at work, or any place else for that matter, why don't we take breathing breaks just as frequently? The good news is that we never leave home without our breath. Whether we use the method that says to tighten our stomach muscles and push our chin forward as we exhale through our mouth with a loud sigh, repeating it ten times or so, or we choose to breathe in through our mouth and exhale through our mouth, the key is to stop, drop, and breathe. Science has proven that deep inhalation increases oxygen in the blood, and strong breathing out expels carbon dioxide waste from our body. The result is energy so that we can be present to our wants or whatever is our next thing!

8

WHAT'S ANGER GOT
TO DO WITH IT?

*D*epression is more than just a diagnosis; depression becomes the mind's default program. It becomes the way that the body and mind seek to cope in crisis. Depression is the result of a complex set of byproducts affecting the brain, including chemical imbalances, faulty mood regulation by the brain, or genetic vulnerability. I saw this unnamed malaise in my family for at least three generations. It was triggered outwardly, it seemed, from grief, loss of financial stability, diabetes diagnosis, and stress.

Depression happens when brain chemistry is altered by stress left untended, other medical conditions, and even the side effects of medication. Depression can be likened to a home's thermostat going haywire and dropping the normal temperature to drastic and dramatically low temperatures for extended periods of time without relief. There are perhaps as many explanations for a depression diagnosis as there are people diagnosed;

depression is multifactorial. There are so many contributing factors to depression that it can cause heightened frustration when a physician can't pinpoint a single cause.

I came to see that an aspect of my depression was also the result of years of anger stuffed and turned inward, ignored, or swept under the rug for the sake of politeness. I grew up in an era when children were not permitted to have feelings, or so it seemed. It was a common belief that "children should be seen and not heard," so, of course, I assumed any outward display of anger was unacceptable. Now, I don't recall any adult saying that I wasn't allowed to be angry, but it seems to me to have been one of those implied and thus understood rules. Just like it was implied that when we went to visit someone's house and they had plastic on the living room furniture and plastic runners on the carpet, as a kid we were not going to be sitting in that room! No one ever said it, but it was implied.

Looking back, it appears to me that many black adults weren't allowed to express their feelings, either. The statement "If you are mad, you better get glad, or I'll give you something to get mad about" seems to run generations deep. Whether it is a Southern culture thing or a black family thing, I can't say, but I've heard some blacks and some whites say they grew up with the same kind of restrictions on emotions, especially anger. Lil' Juanita took that message in, and it became a rule. My anger went underground. I thought that I would be better off and safer without it.

Mad, Happy, Glad, and Sad

I came to understand that "mad" was taken off of the emotions table. To be mad could cause punishment. For some it had caused death. Remember Cain and Abel? Cain had an anger problem. It drove him to kill his younger brother and caused Cain to be displaced from the land he had known. Anger is no less of an issue today. All we have to do is turn on the television or listen in on social media. Anger in our communities has proven to be a weighty matter and at times all too distressingly tragic for black and brown bodies in America.

I am coming to realize just how much psychological damage has been done to African Americans because of colonialism in America. The system of slavery taught us that we had a limited range of emotion, and we were confined to statements like, "I love you, Master. No, Master, I will not run away." The negation of anger has been paralyzing for our country in varying ways for both the oppressed and the oppressor. I have spoken to women from across the cultural spectrum, and many have echoed the experience of feeling as though they were not allowed to express anger. I thought it was just me.

I am reminded of a dramatic and captivating scene in the epic made-for-television miniseries *Roots* (1977, 2016), where the slave owner tortured Kunta Kinte, a man who had been master of his own fate in Africa, whipping him into submission until he succumbed to being called by the name the slave owner had given him: Toby. Versions of that scene have been carried out in various places around the world, until those brutalized succumbed to the disgrace, the pressure, the humiliation, and the power of the oppressor, whether an employer, an institution, popular culture, or the bullying kids in the schoolyard. The oppressed find themselves silenced, forbidden to speak their truth, to say what they feel, and to have it validated. There is no doubt in my mind that in America we need healing and the therapeutic benefits of anger management training.

Expanding My Emotional Vocabulary

My second therapist, Sue, asked me how I felt. I had experienced a good day, so I responded in my usual pat answer of "I am fine." In the church world, "I am fine" is the equivalent of "I am blessed." It's the standard response that usually allows us to ignore what we are not willing to discuss.

Sue Barnum became my new therapist after my time with my first therapist, Dr. Pittman McGehee, had come to an end. Pittman had seen me through the toughest nine months or so after the crash, and his guidance was tremendously stabilizing for me. Thanks to Pittman I experienced triage and was ready to do the next level of healing work, and Sue Barnum was the older, wiser woman I had longed for in my life.

In that first session, as I sat on Sue's sofa, she threw me a shawl and instructed me to hold it as though it were a baby. Like a good girl I complied, bundling the shawl and holding it in my arms. Sue said, "Now fill that baby with all the emotion you are carrying."

As I sat there, allowing the shawl baby to carry my emotions, tears streamed down my face and would not be restrained. That exercise allowed me to transfer my overload of unacknowledged emotions, all the ones that DNA, culture, and life in America had commanded me to block, stuff, and ignore.

Later I told my psychiatrist, Dr. Shana Lee, about the experience. She suggested that I consider expanding my emotional vocabulary. That experience prompted me to search the internet for feeling words. I was blown away. There are lists, graphs, charts, and posters displaying hundreds of words for feelings. To think that I had been held hostage to *glad*. There before me was a plethora of beautiful, heart-tingling, gut-wrenching words that were available to me. I copied one of the lists and kept it in my journal to grow my emotional vocabulary beyond my childhood understanding of what was acceptable. This is what fosters emotional intelligence.

I am ready to grow up into the woman—spirit, mind, body, and emotions—God longs for me to be. I don't have to remain in the limiting mindset of childhood. First Corinthians 13:11 offers a glimpse into liberation: "When I was a child, I spoke like a child, I thought like a child, I reasoned like a child; when I became an adult, I put an end to childish ways" (NRSV).

Angry Black Woman?

Sue taught me that depression is anger turned inward. Anger tells us that something is wrong, but it is our work to identify what that something is.

In his book *The Inward Journey*, Howard Thurman penned these poignant words: "But when knowledge comes, the whole world is turned upside down. The meaning of things begins to emerge. And more importantly, the relations between things are seen for the first time. Questions are asked and answers are sought." I never thought of myself as an angry black woman, especially as the media often likes to portray our women, yet depression had me asking questions I had never asked before.

- Aren't black people regarded as fully human by now?
- When will we be allowed the full range of emotional expression in public or in private? When will we be deemed angry with a just cause?
- When will our pain be acknowledged as post-traumatic slave syndrome?

- When will we be allowed to experience the stages of grief and mourn out loud and have a day proclaimed to close the stores and bring the flags to half-staff because we are living with perpetual mortal anguish?

Thurman wrote that the process is one of moving from innocence to knowledge, which is an unending process. I can sense this shift in me.

My childhood inner world had been couched in a fairy tale, happily-ever-after ending—no real strife or ugly stuff to contend with. I had lived to avoid pain and punishment. But I learned to "put an end to childish ways." While acknowledging the anger that I stuffed has been painful at best, the realization has brought with it a measure of hope.

I am, as Thurman wrote, seeing "for the first time." So yes, I am an angry black woman at times, but one who is learning to live with anger and all that it teaches me. I don't have to be limited by society's attempt to classify me as an angry black woman. I now see that anger is an agent of change.

Sue recommended the book *The Dance of Anger* as a tool for me going forward. She ended that session by saying, "Juanita, the growth for you happens once you begin to allow yourself to feel without judgment."

Later I wrote in my journal:

Sue Barnum had been asking me the kind of probing questions that didn't allow me to ignore the vines. She asked me one particular visit to "notice what angers you." She invited me to reflect in my journal using these statements. How might I have stated my need more clearly? How can I stay present to my feelings and honor them if I do not pay attention to them? "Juanita, be direct and make yourself heard to push yourself into action." She reminded me that it is my job to become a good communicator, to say what I need because no one can read my mind. Funny, I often felt those who really loved me should be able to read my mind.

Lord, have mercy. It was clear I had so much work to do. This woman was asking me to learn how to be with my feelings. It seemed so foreign to me. But *The Dance of Anger* was starting to resonate with me as it talked about patterns of protecting the other person by "keeping the relationship calm." For my mother, and her father before her, the vines—all the ways we learn and pattern behavior—are real and the roots run deep. Clearly, I had learned this pattern as a child, and it too would come to be undone as I continued to seek knowledge and pay attention to my behavior.

PAUSE TO REFLECT

My dear friend Debbie Wilson said to me recently, "Anger pinpoints pain." I had never heard that phrase before. Her words were poignant as she sat processing her grief at the passing of her beloved husband Joe.

Sit with your most recent experience of anger. Give yourself permission to explore it. Write down, perhaps in a journal, what triggered your anger. What troubled you about that trigger? What was your response; how did you react to your feelings of anger? Now hold up to God the things that the person or institution did to you. Name what has upset you. Go to The Work of Byron Katie (thework. com/instruction-the-work-byron-katie) and complete the "Judge Your Neighbor" worksheet. Allow space for God's grace and truth to be revealed to you.

The Psalms are filled with the full range of human emotions. The angry psalms are called "imprecatory" in that they curse and often invoke evil on one's enemy. They send a clear message to us that God is more than capable of being with us in our anger and more than willing to convert the anger into fuel for change. Often the change is the transformation needed to bring about our individual and collective healing of consciousness. Read one of the imprecatory psalms, such as Psalm 69, 109, or 140, and then write an angry psalm of your own. At the end of your psalm turn your anger over to God and ask for God's guidance. Close your writing time with a few minutes of listening for God to speak to you. Journal what you sense, feel, or believe, and notice what God seems to be saying to you or offering you as a gift from this practice.

Some of us have such a difficult experience with anger that we may need training to manage our anger and to identify the gifts of anger that can compel us toward transformational change in our thinking and behavior. Remember that God longs for our deepening awareness and more expansive way of being representatives of God's love in the world.

I mentioned that depression can be a result of avoiding our anger. Richard Rohr has written on anger in his book *Oneing: An Alternative Orthodoxy*. Rohr offers a balanced approach to the subtle distinctions of anger and its necessary and helpful aspects. Please give yourself permission to take however long is needed for you to hear the honest message of your anger and to begin the healing work. As another dear friend, Ava Graves, has said, "No one can tell you how long you need to grieve." I'll add that no one can tell you how long you will need to explore your anger. There is a distinct difference in having a feeling of anger and being controlled by it.

Interlude

DEPRESSION'S WARNING SIGNS

When asked by my friend Cynthia Clay Briggs if there were signs leading up to the depression, I can point to the day Anita called me for an appointment. As her pastor, I assumed she needed to talk with me about a concern of hers. Little did I know that her concern was for me.

Anita is a tall, attractive woman about five years younger than me. As we took our seats in the church's overflow section, she thanked me for the appointment and went straight to the point. "Pastor Juanita, the Lord told me to meet with you to let you know that you are depressed." She admitted to having been reluctant to meet with me, yet wanting to be obedient to God.

I was taken aback, needless to say, never having experienced anyone coming to me on behalf of God with a health diagnosis. As a pastor I'm often on guard when someone comes to me and says, "Thus saith the Lord." So I didn't quite know what to do with her announcement. After assuring her that I didn't feel depressed, I told her thank you, and that I appreciated her time and concern.

It wasn't long afterward that I would experience the magnitude of Anita's message. Perhaps I should have asked more questions that day like, "What should I do about this?" On some level I knew the truth of Anita's words. For months I would come to worship service and cry incessantly. Because of that, one of my colleagues, Rev. Jini Kilgore Ross, called me Jeremiah the weeping prophet! She only half-jokingly reminded me of how Jeremiah in the Old Testament had wept for the people of God as he spoke truth to them.

St. John's Church is the kind of place where the broken and bruised show up for hope and healing. I often say that St. John's is like a hospital. People come in through the emergency room door in varying states of crisis. Our team works diligently to triage those we can. This work is grueling. Misery can take a toll after a while, leading to what's known as compassion fatigue. All too common among those in the various helping professions, it's akin to burnout.

Our emergency room rarely closes long enough for the staff to exhale, let alone to be reinvigorated. Rudy and I are workaholics, which no doubt is infused into the culture. We often half laugh at how one of our ties as a couple has been our collective family history of having a solid work ethic. That said, neither of us has known what it means to take a break or a sabbath for ourselves. When Anita made her announcement, we hadn't had a vacation; it had been seven years at the helm of a rapidly moving ministry.

It's my practice to stay upbeat and never let anyone see me sweat. But my tears would leak out in worship. When I entered the sanctuary, I felt the pain and the presence of the Spirit. I didn't realize that sheer exhaustion was mixed in as well. Perhaps it would have been wise for me to have taken the time to be with Anita's message. Now I know that, but hindsight is 20/20.

9

LETTING GO OF JUDGMENT

I was in my car listening to a CD by Wayne Dyer as he told the story of chauffeuring his daughter and her friends to the mall. The girls began to talk poorly of another girl they knew.

He asked them, "Who will defend her?"

They replied, "What are you talking about?"

Dyer asked, "Who will speak on her behalf?" He then declared that he would represent her. The girls became silent and quickly changed the subject, because their little "game" of judgment was brought into the light.

Was this uncomfortable? You bet it was! But discomfort is what we must feel if we are to be aware of our actions and make the necessary corrections. Judgment keeps us from seeing the good in another. This is the foundation for marginalizing the other. Jesus understood this when he confronted the men who were ready to stone the woman caught in adultery (John 8).

There are so many questions to be asked about that strange scene. Who caught her? How did they catch her? Who was her companion in the act? Wasn't he also guilty? Did he set her up? Why was the woman not given a proper trial? I hadn't seen judgment and finger pointing as a source of marginalization until I listened to Dyer's CD. The questions raised caused a light to come on for me and helped me see how I had pointed my fingers judgmentally just like the girls in the car.

Am I a Pharisee?

I never realized how easily I judged people until I was in recovery from the crash. I would have made one hell of a Pharisee. I was a perpetual rule follower who feared punishment from authority figures like my father. Rules for children are designed to provide them with a measure of safety and to teach impulse control, whereas for adults those same rules can become a means by which another is judged.

Judging others was a way to make me feel better about myself; I can see that now. It allowed me to focus on what others were doing wrong so I could feel justified as a Christian and could check things off my "doesn't do" list—a list all Pharisees have in their heads, which sounds like, "Well, I would never do that. How could he do that? They are horrible because they did that," and so on.

Judgment infers that someone is wrong and someone else is right. And because I'm following Jesus, I must be right. Many believers in Jesus tend to think belief in Christ gives them the right to judge. But if I have one finger pointing at someone, there are three fingers pointing back at me. So, what real invitation did this awareness of judgment bring to my life? Was it to check the boxes off? Juanita plays well with others—check.

Juanita follows the rules—check. Those checks prove that Juanita must be a good girl, which means she gets the coveted "Get into Heaven Free" card!

No, I was being invited through this new awareness to take a good, long look at myself, but not in comparison to others. That's what Jesus did in John 8 when he told the male accusers gathered around the woman caught in adultery—*drum roll please*—"Let any one of you who is without sin be the first to throw a stone at her" (v. 7). Jesus' words must have felt like a boomerang bouncing off the conscience of each man present. I too know that feeling. It is mind blowing to me just how long I have lived unconscious of my way of seeing life and relationships. Lord, have mercy. Come to think of it, the crash probably is the mercy I needed.

How often have I stood before others in this insanely wounded world wanting to cast the first stone? *Her skirt is too short. His pants are too low. What kind of home did they come from that they don't know better than that?* Rounds and rounds of judgment, like skeet shooters waiting for the next clay target and the thrill of yelling, "Pull!" My words have been ammunition in conversations like the one Wayne Dyer's daughter and her friends had, conversations that killed the reputation of another person. I had never seen my actions as being so vile, violent, and disturbing until after the crash. What had seemed normal was now small-minded, and I regretted my immaturity. Most times it wasn't said. But my thoughts had that person arrested, tried, and convicted. This was all rooted in a childhood pattern of being right, being a good girl.

A dynamic happens in a group that changes the chemistry of the people in the circle so they become more vicious than they would on their own. Don't we see it when individuals trample one another during the Black Friday sales before Christmas? It's the same mob mentality that is captured by the news networks while we sit at home thinking, *I would never do something like that.* The reality is, many of us stand in a circle with stones in hand all too often.

At root, the men who stood like a mob around the woman caught in adultery needed to feel superior. But deep down, they were wounded little boys who were exercising the only power they knew. Comparison and judgment are based on feelings of inadequacy and powerlessness. In this powerless mindset, we make choices in order to regain control. If I'm busy pointing the finger at someone, then that person might not call out my deficiencies. My places of vulnerability can remain hidden and unchecked. This kind of thinking highlights why someone like Hitler was able to gain power and no one called his bluff. Why? Because of the mob mentality.

In John 8, Jesus went directly to the root of the problem: sin. Who among you has not sinned also? When you sinned, who was there to stone you? When you turned away from the way of love, who set you up? What powerful cartel was ready to pounce on you because you blew it? Did the fear of failing cause you to sabotage your success? Fear of success? Was it guilt from not living up to your own expectations? Jesus stood up for this woman and freed her, but he also freed the men from the guilt and shame they might have felt for killing this woman. He freed the men to look at themselves and to see themselves perhaps for the first time.

Jesus then wrote something on the ground that the Bible does not reveal. Maybe he wrote, *Let go of your need to be right* or

Let go of your need to make someone wrong. Somewhere between Jesus' challenging statement and what he wrote, there was time enough for the men to reflect on their actions.

I've learned since the crash to take more time to reflect on who I am. While I can play the game of "I don't do this or that," it is only a childish cover-up for what I actually do. What's going on in my heart and mind? What am I unwilling to face about myself that makes it easier for me to stand in the mob than to defend people I judge?

When I read the book *Don't Forgive Too Soon* by Dennis Linn, Sheila Fabricant Linn, and Matthew Linn, it came to me that whether I am the woman caught or the men caught in John 8, I was still in the circle. A word from the Lord, however, could free me, as it freed the woman to "go your way, and from now on do not sin again" (John 8:11 NRSV). Reflecting on this truth, however, was my work to do. I could discern my notions of sin and define it as all the ways I operate separately from God, allowing my passions to rule me instead of allowing God to transform and grow me. Jesus is always ready to help us grow up beyond our useless childhood ways of being. He is not interested in systems of thinking and belief that stamp our behavior as okay and allow us to get away with murder, literally or figuratively.

Judgment has an energy that is not life-giving for anybody. When I live in judgment instead of the truth, something within me dies. Often that something is compassion for myself and ultimately compassion for others. Even in my suffering, I do not have to demonize or degrade those who do not live the way that I think matters. When I'm awake to doing my own growing, my transformational work, I hear Jesus say, "Let any one of you who is without sin be the first to throw a stone." I stand watching as he writes on the tablet of my heart and frees me to leave the mob scene, to go and sin no more. Had I not listened as Jesus spoke, I would not have gained my freedom, the freedom that comes when I let go of my propensity to judge the other. My freedom is twofold because I'm more aware now that the first person I routinely judged was myself. I realize that Jesus is freeing me from my own internal critic. I can choose to lay down my mistaken belief that I have some kind of right to judge. I set others free, and I learn to set myself free too.

Depression is anger turned inward, and judging is an unnecessary means of holding on to anger. Judgment and resentment are kindling for anger; they go hand in hand. Each of them is capable of destroying the good that God longs to bring to life in us. A judging and critical attitude blocks our flow of goodness. We often have set ideas about how we think good will come into our lives. When I judge others, it is my ego saying, "Nope, that one can't bless me," and "Nope, not that one either." I discount how God wants to use those people in my life for our mutual good. I have limited myself by assuming that I know it all and don't need the support of others on my life journey.

As a kid, my ego helped me construct a meaning for my experiences with the people in my life. It drew from limited insight and worked to gather evidence to decide who was in, who was out, and what the rules were for living. *Oh, she's out for sure,* my ego would say. *Did you see the way she folded her arms? She folded them just like your old teacher, so she's probably just like your old teacher.* My ego would gather evidence and see patterns and then use them to allow me to condemn the other person. But God has invited me into a new way—a richer, fuller, less hollow way of being.

In our Renovaré gatherings I routinely heard Dallas Willard say, "The chief aim of God in all of history is the creation of an all-inclusive community of loving persons with God as chief sustainer and most glorious inhabitant." By judging folks all these years, my ego built a case for or against them based on sketchy data. If I pronounced them innocent, I permitted them access to the gate I kept watch over (because my righteousness was as the scribes and Pharisees), which would allow them entrance to that community. On the other hand, if I found them guilty, I condemned them to eternal doom because their way of being in the world didn't line up with my unrealistic expectations. And heck, those expectations were unrealistic for me, so how could I think they were realistic for anyone else?

The only two fights I got into in elementary school (and got the stuffing beat out of me) were because I had judged two girls who wouldn't tolerate my judgment. There were bullies in school. I wasn't a bully, but there should be a category for Pharisees in training. That was me. Righteousness ought not to have a certain condemning tone or a look that reduces a person to nothingness. Yet I did that as a child and way too long as an adult.

The crash invited me to let go of ways of being that don't line up with the all-inclusive community God is seeking to build. It helped to shake me free from my masks, to acknowledge my anger, and let down the walls that were keeping God's love from flowing freely through me. As long as I walked in judgment of others, I was holding myself in judgment and limiting God to a role as judge and condemner.

It's taken a while, but I am seeing that the crash was not just about depression but about spiritual awakening, spiritual transformation. God was helping me see that living out of a place of judgment was rooted in judging myself, a byproduct of the past that was to be left in the past.

In this new life God offered, I am grounded in the vast inclusiveness of God's love and mercy. This is now the source of my life rather than demeaning comparisons and brutal condemnation that we Pharisees are really good at in the name of Jesus. I, like the men surrounding the woman caught in adultery, was being invited to let go of all thoughts and ways of being that no longer served me. These thoughts and behaviors had made up the essence of who I had believed myself to be at my very core. God was allowing me to see, maybe for the first time in my life, because God really had my attention now. I could see clearly how a lifetime of my thoughts and beliefs had built the life that had crashed and shattered so devastatingly on August 27.

When I'm tempted to judge someone or a situation, I'm being invited to ask myself, *Why do I think what I'm thinking? What am I feeling? How do I act when I think this way? What is the truth here?* Jesus constantly invites us into a more expansive way of being. I now realize how my childhood program for happiness was one with limiting beliefs about my life and my world. God invited me into the deep ocean of joy, peace, contentment, compassion, and self-value. But I was bound by a childhood view that was more like a teaspoon of water in comparison, a teaspoon of water I was afraid to spill out of dread of the punishment that would no doubt come about.

My childhood happiness program was filled with all manner of judgments about others. I see now how those people were simply actors revealing aspects of me that I couldn't see. Carl Jung calls this our shadow. It's part of what the Palmores called the you that you don't see but that others see with glaring accuracy.

Scripture speaks about those of us who have perfect vision for seeing the specks in the eyes of others, which is amazing considering that we have a wooden two-by-four plank in our own eyes. The people I judged were simply bringing my shadow into living color. I'm seeing that what irritates me in others is often a message more about me than them. When I take the time to be with the irritation, I understand more about myself. When I see, then I can heal.

The depression has offered me enough space to see and to think through my beliefs and their impact on my life. How generous is God's love for me and for others? I had for so long been caught up in the rules I had collected in childhood that I didn't see the loving relationship God had been yearning for me to experience.

PAUSE TO REFLECT

What habit or action have you routinely seen in others that has disturbed you or has caused you to point the finger in judgment or blame?

Sit with your "plank." Journal how it is inviting you to pay attention to what's happening in you that creates this discord or disdain for others. Look again at The Work of Byron Katie (thework.com/instruction-the-work-byron-katie) and complete the "One Belief at a Time" worksheet.

Add color to your life. The crash helped me see my need for colors that energized me. During the darkest days following the crash, my husband and daughters began a painting project that turned our house into a canvas exploding with the brilliance of a Caribbean sunrise: oranges, yellows, and reds. Guests often commented on Rudy's uninhibited use of color and how they thought of taking risks with color in their own homes after seeing our now brilliantly hued abode.

Rudy later told me that his choice of colors was his subconscious way of bringing back the color and joy that I had brought to our family and home. His use of color brought subtle rays of hope into our home as we learned to live in the aftermath of the crash.

How has color enhanced your mood in the past? How might you consider adding color to your world? Perhaps it could be flowers or a throw cover or just a brightly colored shirt. You might try experimenting with color and see if it offers positive effects on your overall mood.

10

CLAIMING A NEW IDENTITY

When I was seventeen, my father decided it was time to give me the big picture of his insurance business. After he explained it to me, I thought, *Hey, I can do that*. And I did. From that day until the day I married Rudy, I worked in my father's business and was the top producer most of that time. He was vocal, commanding, and strong, and I wanted to be just like my daddy.

I have been a walking contradiction for as long as I can remember. I tried to be my father's high-performance son and a good little girl at the same time. No wonder I had trouble figuring out who I was! I also wanted to share in the power my father wielded as he made decisions, gave directions to people, and earned the respect of many who knew him. He was in control, and I was determined to be in control of my life too.

I knew a number of other young women who went into business with their fathers. All of us longed for words of praise and affirmation from our dads, and we were driven to earn those words.

Pressed into a Mold

Consider a baby girl being born. The nurses clean that crying child, comfort her, and then present her to the proud parents. One of them pronounces, "She'll do just great!" Not "she'll *be* just great," but "she'll *do* just great." That minutes-old little person is shackled with expectations of performance. To complicate matters, the mother and the father have very different pictures of their daughter's future. The mother imagines a priceless doll admired for her beauty. The father sees a future CEO.

As the girl grows up, she loves to paint and dance. Her mother wants her to play tea party, and her father pushes her to be the captain of her soccer team. Neither of them, however, recognizes and values the little girl's God-given passions for art and dance. Over the years the mother grows impatient with the girl's preoccupation with the arts, and the little girl's father keeps pushing her to excel in a sport she really doesn't care for. But eventually the girl learns to tolerate her mother's insistence on quiet talks around tea, and she becomes a pretty good soccer player. Both parents want her to be successful, but neither looks into her heart to see what motivates her.

She goes to college on a soccer scholarship and gets a great job in a corporation. Her parents are so proud. But years later the dissonance between her heart's desires and the expectations of her parents create such tension that she experiences physical symptoms of stress. She's outwardly successful and seems to have life by the tail, but she's depressed. Daily she pushes through panic attacks and body aches; she is listless, empty, and unable to concentrate; she feels hopelessness and despair; and she has no interest in the things that had once given her real joy.

A wise doctor refers her to a therapist who digs deep into her soul and finds that the real person has been squeezed into the mold of her parents' expectations her entire life, and now it's time for the real person to emerge.

This situation is hypothetical, but the symptoms are all too common. As I see it, all of us need to be loved for who we are, not for who others expect us to be. Each of us needs to figure out how to be the person God created us to be, a person with gifts, talents, and desires that enable us to first *be* and then *do* our life with a sense of security, passion, and joy.

Many of us are so busy doing what others want us to do that we never find out who we really are. The result is that we are dying inside, and we burn out because we're only performing instead of expressing our heart's desires in our actions all day, every day. To the degree that we let others dictate our lives, we become frazzled, discouraged, depressed, or worse.

To compensate for our insecurities, most of us wear masks. We wear a mask of competence to impress people, a mask of intimidation to control them with our anger, a mask of defensiveness to keep people from hurting us again, and a mask with a painted-on smile so people won't see the pain we're trying to hide. Finding our identities means taking off these masks, a process that, to our ego, threatens to expose us as frauds but promises to give us a rich, honest sense of self and can result in far more meaningful relationships based on truth, not fiction.

Our search for our identity, however, isn't a license for irresponsible choices. For example, I've heard some people go through a midlife crisis and pronounce, "Now that I understand who I am, I'm going to divorce my partner and find somebody who really gets me." Our identity is a complicated thing. Trading off the old relationship for a new one isn't necessarily the answer. We can balance and blend our heart's desires and responsibilities. All of us have made commitments, and we still need to fulfill those if at all possible as we pursue the things that bring us joy and life. The individual can transform and so can relationships; I have seen this transformation take place.

For me, finding my true self clarified what really mattered to me and cleared away tons of distractions that had kept me from living into who I am. I am clear that my chief responsibility is to be true to discovering the me God and I are co-creating together. Instead of being so driven to achieve, I began to practice being more present to myself, Rudy, and the girls. Instead of being preoccupied with all the "important things" I had to say, I began to value what others thought and said, and I am learning to listen; some days are better than others. Instead of feeling like I had to perform to win the approval of every human being who ever lived, I began to relax and give myself breathing space to enjoy my encounters, and to focus on things that really matter, like memorable moments. My editor, Cindy Bunch, introduced me to the Danish word *hygge*. It's the practice of taking the time to slow down and enjoy the simplicity of friends, family, and the things of our lives in a cozy sort of way. So, I'm learning *hygge*.

Awakening to Live

A big part of the transformation of my identity was to be objective about the darkness in my life. I've lived most of my life in fear: fear of losing control, fear of failure, fear of punishment, criticism, and being exposed as not good enough. But that fear came from an even deeper problem: inadequacy.

Inadequacy emerges from false beliefs that create a sense of feeling worthless, hopeless, and powerless. It's not just "I have to meet others' standards," but "*I* am not enough." To compensate, I tried to be powerful, always right, in control, and worthy of ultimate respect. But it was all a charade, a game I didn't know consciously I was playing. Striving to win approval and acceptance was exhausting. The aftermath of the crash has illuminated those wrong beliefs and false notions. Out of the darkness truth came to the light. I found a new source of identity from being open to receiving God's love, and feeling loved without having to do a darn thing has made me open to loving me for me. Now loving others comes easier, and there is so much joy in being myself without the weighty and tiresome burden of wearing a mask. I am learning to accept my personality and my God-given abilities and use them with wholehearted joy—not misusing them to gain approval from people.

In the search for my true identity, I'm learning to exercise and celebrate my uniqueness, my own way of being in the world. By nature I'm a risk-taker. As I've been growing, changing, expanding, it's really transforming me in wildly wonderful ways. I've been willing to do some things that in the past I wouldn't have done because they would have threatened the approval of others, but the new me is going for it. I realize now that I had turned my power over to all the people I was seeking approval from. God was teaching me how to be the authority in my own queendom, the queen of my own being. It felt like I was breathing for the first time in a long time. I was learning how to be me.

The crash has taught me that a secure identity comes from our relationship with God. The apostle John identified himself in his Gospel as "the disciple whom Jesus loved" (John 13:23).

Does that mean he was the only one Jesus loved? Of course not. It means that Christ's warm, strong, grace-filled acceptance was so overwhelming to John that it determined his very identity. It can determine ours too.

God doesn't love us because we've earned it. Quite the opposite. That's what grace is about! God opens wide the kingdom for God's children, who are "dearly loved" (Colossians 3:12) and precious to God. Self-esteem doesn't come by telling ourselves a million times that we are worthy, although that doesn't hurt. Rather, it's developed as we grasp the startling truth that God, in magnificent, benevolent, and wildly outrageous grace, loves us. I am growing more open to and seeing in fresh new ways how "some things [like great art, poetry, and music] are loved because they are worthy"—they possess an appreciable value—"and some things are worthy because they are loved." You and I fall into the latter category.

Does that mean we sit on our butts and do nothing because we've been unconditionally accepted? Not at all. The grace of God energizes us and directs us to do two things: humbly give thanks and boldly take action. The more we integrate God's grace into our hearts and heads, the freer we become from our childhood happiness programs, and we'll stop re-creating our victimizing beliefs and instead be known for our hearts of gratitude and our glad acts of service. We'll be present in the world out of a spaciousness that is far-reaching and life-giving to us and those around us as well. Some will not understand, but that is their work to do.

Our *doing*, no longer bound to the impositions of others' opinions or expectations, will spring out of our deep and inexhaustible well of *being*.

Identity as a Treasure

Replacing feelings of inadequacy, fear, and worthlessness with truth, honesty, and confidence has changed my world. This has been the work of the Spirit of God in me; it was God-initiated, God's way of awakening me to live. The darkness had a way of annihilating everything my ego identity valued. The darkness, the long shadow of silence and solitude, made way for the crushing weight of ego identification to be dismantled, literally smashed. Nothing that I had previously valued as being me— my accomplishments or even my failures, my roles, my to-do list—remained; it all crumbled. In the darkness of the crash I came to know nothing save the awareness of a deep, loving union with God and God revealing me to myself.

It's kind of like coming home to find out that all of our prized possessions have turned to ash, and we can see them for what they were: nothing. Oddly there is no sadness or grief in seeing that; actually, there is so much relief and gratitude. I'm thankful that there is now more space for what can be and the clear awareness that my life is distinctly simple, not the complex self I had known; this insight has been amazingly refreshing and life-giving. All that defined me has been removed and replaced with a new reality. My sense of self is being revealed to me sometimes in the course of a day or a week. But the revelation comes. Now I know the crash had to happen so that the treasures so deeply embedded in me that were hidden from my sight could be revealed. Only this recovery time and space and mining effects of the crash could have excavated them.

The parable in Matthew 13, in which the man finds treasure in a field then sells all he has to buy the field, makes perfectly good sense to me. The treasure that I am coming to see in me is worth surrendering all that I had believed about myself. The old me feels like fool's gold in comparison to the state of transcendence that I have been experiencing. I am growing in my awareness of my own sense of *being*; the presence of God in me is all-affirming. The cords of attachment are falling away, and I feel no compulsion to do anything or any need to have work or affirmations to validate me; I just am. I'm clear that God is in this, allowing the flow of God's love along with this profound awareness that *I am*. Nothing to earn, nothing to accomplish, nothing to justify or to validate. I am because God is. Psalm 46:10 invites stillness as a means of knowing God: "Be still, and know that I am God!" (NRSV). I am growing to appreciate that in the stillness God, who is the "I am," is revealed and made known, and likewise I am coming to know the me who is as well. This is being born again for me from above and from within.

Steps Toward a New Sense of Identity

Psychologists identify unhealthy behavior that springs from a false self. They point out that wearing masks leads to all kinds of maladaptive coping behaviors, such as trying to dominate, running from intimacy out of fear, wallowing in self-pity, and shading the truth (lying) to keep others from knowing who we really are.

French philosopher and mathematician Blaise Pascal observed this human tendency to live apart from reality. In his book *Pensées*, Pascal wrote, "We labor unceasingly to preserve an imaginary existence and neglect the real." Clinging to an imaginary existence raises our expectations as it divorces us from reality, leaving us vulnerable to the twin problems of overreaching pride, demanding to be the center of attention, and a victim mentality that's never satisfied.

In our self-absorbed world, one of the chief problems I've seen is misappropriated pride that results in self-pity. Pride and self-pity are alternate sides of the same coin. They devastate our relationships with God and others. Numerous studies and books illustrate how our culture has drifted (or sprinted) toward a victim mentality in the past few decades. Social scientist Daniel Yankelovich's book *New Rules: Searching for Self-Fulfillment in a World Turned Upside Down* discusses how we've shifted from self-sacrifice in a post-World War II era to self-indulgence today. In his book *A Nation of Victims*, Charles Sykes, a journalist and political commentator, reports that the rise in litigation stems from our self-perception as victims. We sue at the slightest provocation to get what we think we deserve. Seeing ourselves as victims leads directly to self-pity.

The Need for Approval

Growing up with a serious addiction to approval means that I have unknowingly engaged in a lot of blaming, complaining, and explaining. All these are merely ways of distancing myself from punishment or the fear of being unaccepted. As God is revealing me to me, I've realized I no longer have to rely on blaming, complaining, or explaining to justify my humanity or my being. I no longer need to use these as a means for acquiring acceptance or approval. So, my motto is "Don't blame, don't complain, and don't explain"—each of these are justifications for behavior and serve as poor defense mechanisms. I notice now that my energy level lowers when I resort to these addictive measures.

Letting go of these spells freedom from self-pity, but getting there means letting go of my need to be accepted. Explanations are about justifying myself to others. Now I know that I can live with the emotional discomfort that inevitably happens when stuff in my life appears to fall apart. I don't have to point the finger at anyone else for the choices I do or don't make.

I'm also learning the new freedom that comes—even while my stomach churns in rebellion—as I abandon my old script of asking, *What will people think?* They will think whatever they think, and I will go on and so will they. I have come to realize that I'm just not that important, that my absence will not cause the great chaos that my ego had convinced me of. I can choose to make my self-interest a priority in any matter. I can choose what's best for me and my well-being without blaming, complaining, or explaining away my choices. This is another way women, in particular, give their power away and end up carrying unnecessary weights and burdens.

Over the years my husband has exercised great freedom in this area while I have wrestled between self-care and other-centered activities. I've drowned myself in "I really should do this or that or the other." *Should* is all about other people's expectations and narratives for my life.

I recall a therapy session or two when I was asked to identify who was behind my *I should.* My family, my friends, my parents, my teachers, my mentors, my faith tradition—it was overwhelming to call all those witnesses into question regarding their input in my decisions about where to go or what to do, or even something as specific as whether to take a long, hot soak! If I didn't want their input about my decision to soak in the tub, then why was I giving them so much freedom to pull my strings in my day-to-day decisions? Those sessions made me realize I had some work to do to understand myself and my motivations.

The Enneagram has been an amazing tool in allowing me to see my blind spots, like my need for approval and my deep dependence on blaming, complaining, explaining, and perfection. Consider reviewing your Enneagram number. How have you self-identified? Which of those ways of being are you unaware of, yet others have noticed in you? I invite you to be still and know "I am." Start journaling what you have identified as areas that need new awareness, attention, and transformation.

I had to pay attention to how often I said out loud and internally, "I should." What are you saying to yourself that feeds into an identity that no longer serves you? How does your inner critic attempt to control, demean, or bully you? Write it down. Then consider writing yourself a note about what your life might look like without those pesky ways of thinking about yourself.

11

HAVE-TO VERSUS WANT-TO

J showed up at my psychiatrist's office—the inner sanctum, if you will—and dropped like lead onto the sofa, sighing deeply. My sighs were not sarcastic—sighs had become my words. You know how Romans 8:26 says that the Holy Spirit interprets even our moans and our groans? My sighs were too deep for words. I hoped God was getting my message.

The sunlight shone on the terraced porch outside Dr. Shayna Lee's windows. The office was a cottage in the Third Ward area of Houston. It was soothing, quaint, and homey yet functional. It had charts showing the brain—the flow of the nervous system—and personal mementos that made me realize that outside of her work, she too had a life. Somehow that was comforting.

There in the waiting room was a cross section of Houston: people like me who perhaps never expected to be living with a mental health crisis, an old-school grandmother training her grandkids to "behave in this office," someone who was dropped off in a cab, someone else who arrived in a flashy sports car. There we were—all needing some relief from our mental woes. I had the sense that Dr. Lee, a black female psychiatrist, understood where we all came from.

She stepped into the room and with a warm smile said, "Mrs. Rasmus, good to see you again," as though we were old friends. I guess that beat being old enemies.

She asked about the medication I was taking that she had prescribed. After I reported that I didn't seem to feel any better with the medication, she said what she undoubtedly said a hundred times or more each week: "The medication has to get into your system. It's a one-day-at-a-time process. It will take time—typically six weeks, sometimes sooner, sometimes a little later. But remember: this crisis that you are coming back from has been occurring unreported within your system for a while. Be patient with yourself as we move through this process together."

I sighed again deeply. I knew she'd heard me.

After we discussed the medication, she asked about Rudy and the girls—how they seemed to be coping with my depression. When I called it a nervous breakdown, she quickly informed me that the term *nervous breakdown* could not be found in the *Diagnostic and Statistical Manual.* Rather, I was diagnosed with a major depressive episode.

I was too depleted to say, "Whoopee! So, it's not called a nervous breakdown?" The sigh that followed could be interpreted as sarcasm.

Maybe correcting the medical terminology was her way of dispelling some of the myths I had about nervous breakdowns and crazy women doing crazy things and being locked up. Actually, I was perfectly fine with the term. I had heard it used in hushed tones by my grandmother or my parents as a little girl. It didn't frighten me, really. While I was indeed sick, I wasn't callous or emotionally abusive, as best as I could tell. Some things only become clear over time, but I have tried to be a good mom.

But after the crash I felt like a zombie, void of any emotions. I can only imagine what people feel like who have lost their memory. How disorienting it must be to awaken with no knowledge of who you are, who you've loved, or who has loved you. In the same way I was surrounded by those I loved while feeling totally empty of all feeling. I felt like a character in a Madame Tussauds Wax Museum—in the right place with the right costume and props but lifeless, as though my soul had been evacuated. I couldn't feel the joy I once felt when Rudy, the girls, and I would laugh and talk after church or the sense of belonging I had known as a wife and mother.

Return to Childhood

Dr. Lee asked, "Mrs. Rasmus, what is it that you really want to do? What do *you* want?" She gave me space to answer. Thinking about her question, I felt as though I had lost something but had no idea what it was. Was this what going insane was like?

I couldn't recall the last time anyone besides a waiter in a restaurant asked what I wanted. I felt panicked. I needed to find this thing that I knew must be hidden in the house of my mind somewhere. Was it buried under a to-do list? Everything in me wanted to scream, "Somebody help! I've lost my want-to!"

In the midst of my flurry of internal searching, Dr. Lee softly said, "I believe that as you move through this recovery, it is going to be important for you to answer that question." I nodded, and we concluded the fifteen-minute check-in.

I drove myself home in a blur. Once in the house, I sat in my favorite chair, stared out of the living room window, and asked God, "How do I find out what I want?"

I heard God say, "Go back to your childhood."

Madear's Porch

In the days that followed, I reflected on my childhood. What did I want as a child? What were my dreams and desires? What did I enjoy imagining?

After a while I remembered how I loved climbing the steps of my grandmother's front porch. She had a porch that should have had large carved lions on each side of the steps like the houses rich white folks had. It was great. I would climb what I called the seats where her lions should have been resting to protect her palace and then jump off into my Superwoman stance. Oh, how I loved to do that! Remembering it almost brought a smile to my face, though my lips weren't cooperating.

When I wasn't climbing those majestic steps, I was climbing her chinaberry tree. How she would lovingly scold me, her firstborn grandchild, "Juanita, stop climbing in that tree before you fall and break your neck!" I don't remember anything about climbing that tree that felt dangerous in the least. I loved that tree and the freedom I felt as I conquered it.

Reflecting on my childhood allowed me to remember that I used to say, "When I get big, I'm going to go skydiving." I don't recall seeing skydivers as a child, although my parents often tried to expose my sister and me to all sorts of new experiences so we wouldn't limit our world based on what we experienced in a segregated Houston. While I don't remember where I got that idea, I remember saying it out loud a couple of times to some grown folks, probably in an effort to be validated. Instead, I was laughed at and told, "Girl, where you get that idea from? Black folks don't do nothing crazy like that!"

I have a friend who has eight siblings. To stretch her budget in those days, her mom prepared meals that were mostly starches: rice, potatoes—hearty foods that could feed her large family on meager wages. When one of her children asked her why they didn't eat vegetables, her response was, "We don't eat that." To this day my friend doesn't eat vegetables.

So often this kind of "we don't do this" thinking was simply a mechanism for minimizing the hurt that was just steps beyond the front door when we left the imagined safety of our homes as black men and women in the 1960s. I understood it, but that didn't stop the desire in my heart for adventure beyond the limits others perceived for me.

The Want-To File

Days after my visit to Dr. Lee, I thought about the want-tos of my life and decided to start a want-to file. I chose pretty pictures that I ripped out of magazines, junk mail, and the sort. I also tore out words that arrested my attention and placed them in the file. Anything that caught my eye: a couple in a hot-air balloon, the poster of a movie I wanted to see, enchanting garden scenes, encouraging words or phrases. I especially appreciated the positive energy from *O, The Oprah Magazine*. While reading was still a chore mentally, I found such life in the vibrant colors of the words and pictures. Even some of Oprah's favorite things were life-giving to look at. My want-to file had become a kind of vision board even though I didn't realize it at the time.

Scripture says that without a vision the people perish. I felt as dead as I could imagine, minus the tombstone and the dirt. I had to believe there would be a resurrection out of that terrible pit. Somehow, my want-to file seemed to give me hope.

Some days I clutched the folder as though it was my passport out of the darkness. There were days, however, when the file meant nothing, but I looked at it anyway. I know a little about how the mind records things both good and bad. I hoped that even though I didn't feel the energy of joy, playfulness, ecstasy, adventure, or confidence reflected by the images in my file, my mind was being infused with those beautiful, hope-filled, life-giving elements, and some good could come out of this practice.

I had a deep sense that my want-to file was about reclaiming my imagination. It seemed to me that the file with its words and images somehow held the key to joy and contentment, new freedom, a new way of being that would replace the old ways of doing life that no longer served me. It seemed as though my want-tos might help me with a redo!

Isn't it crazy that a person has to lose her life to gain it? I think this is what Jesus meant when he talked about laying down our lives (see Matthew 16:24-26). There is no prescription, no instruction for this laying down our old self; it's all on-the-job training. But it was clear to me that I was being invited to lay down my old life and to begin to cultivate the freedom of joy and pleasure.

I have never really thought much about pleasure, at least not as an adult. With all my rule-following and people-pleasing I have been sucking the life out of my soul like people in Texas suck the juices out of the head of a crawfish and then discard it.

How is it that in all that I have read I am just now seeing the need for pleasure and desire? I remember the passage that says that God will give us the desires of our heart if we keep our mind stayed on God (Psalm 37:4), but I was thinking about the serious stuff, the don't-be-damned-to-hell stuff. I never realized that God meant the sweet stuff, the running-around-the-house-in-your-underwear-just-because-you-can stuff. I never recall doing that as a kid, and I was too serious and too busy as an adult. It will be different for my girls, thanks to my friend Elizabeth. We met Elizabeth and her husband, Zack, early on as we started ministry together at St. John's. Elizabeth has always been the God-sent "aunt" from church for our girls. They knew if Rudy and I were out of reach, they could go to Aunt Elizabeth. She allowed our girls the freedom to simply be little girls, something that I have since learned most church folks don't do for the pastor's children. Because of their time with Elizabeth, my girls know about pajama day. Sipping champagne for no special reason or taking a day off from work for your heart's sake, not because you are sick—Elizabeth didn't know it, but she had been teaching us all. Since the crash I began to recognize that grown folks also need to give themselves permission to have pajama day.

Tears clouded my eyes once I reflected on how I had gotten this all wrong. I didn't realize I needed want-tos to fuel my have-tos and gotta-dos. No wonder I had been living on fumes for so long. I had no anticipation of pleasure and joy because I had been living life as a to-do list, checking off the boxes instead of living into imagination and anticipation—the place of sheer childlike joy. I don't believe that it's too late for my girls. I have Elizabeth to thank for that.

Children live what they learn, or at least that's what the sign in the pediatrician's office said. Oh, dear God, please help me get this together so my girls can get this too! I have been trying to do the right thing, to have a good and right life, but I see that I went about it all wrong. I simply didn't know that people-pleasing and approval-seeking and rule-following had been running my life and that they would leave me desperately empty. I was living off of my childhood understanding that "I can get it done; I can do all things." Left to my own devices I have in so many ways left God out, and along with God the joy and pleasure of life. Why didn't somebody tell me that God is cool with me playing, dreaming, imagining, and having fun?

Lance Witt wrote an article that appeared on *Sermon Central*, an online newsletter for pastors, called "The Spiritual Discipline of Anticipation," in which he talks about this spiritual practice that begins with the letter *A*. I gotta say that of all the spiritual disciplines, this one is most foreign to me. There are the disciplines of accountability, abstinence, abject poverty, and I'm sure we can add an *A* to a few more and expand the list. But Witt wrote, "Anticipation is a great word. It is a cousin to expectation, excitement, faith, and suspense. The Merriam-Webster dictionary defines anticipation as 'a feeling of excitement about something that is going to happen, the act of preparing for something.'"

Even today, I realize that my life can be so much richer if I will allow myself to slow down and allow wonder to be cultivated. That is anticipation, that is imagination, and that opens me up to joy and excitement. Anticipation and want-tos seem to be meant for each other, and here all this time I had excommunicated them both.

I am amazed as I reflect on those moments when I was just a step away from the adventure on Madear's porch that caused me to feel unexplainable giddiness and joy, and how deflating it felt to hear my grandmother's words of caution rooted in great love for me, her firstborn grandchild, but likewise rooted in her own great fear. Fear can become the cultural norm for marginalized people. So as a child I heard many warnings, not only from Madear; they were simply in the air I breathed as a child.

One person's fear is another person's sheer delight. Skydiving had been a want-to for all of my life, one that made no sense to anyone but me. Just the thought of it opened my heart so wide that at that moment I felt how painfully closed it had been. I am only now realizing that I have allowed others to claim my voice and my right to the adventures that I dreamed would give me life. Being the compliant rule follower that I have been, I tucked that want-to away, and it didn't come out again until I reflected on my childhood.

In *The Great Omission*, Dallas Willard writes,

> The correct perspective is to see following Christ not only as the necessity it is, but as the fulfillment of the highest human possibilities and as life on the highest plane. It is to see, in Helmut Thielicke's words, that "the Christian stands, not under the dictatorship of a legalistic 'You ought,' but in the magnetic field of Christian freedom, under the empowering of the 'You may.'"

Making my want-to file has made me remember that Madear had a want-to file—a photo album. It had pictures of brick homes and patterns of women's clothing—her dreams and want-tos. She was an incredible seamstress. She made my fabulous fuchsia-colored ball gown and the cap and gown for my kindergarten graduation. I felt so beautiful, like a perfect princess and a scholar. She was incredible, yet she lived most of her life in a state of depression and grief. While she didn't live long enough to see the brick house she longed for, her children and her grandchildren all did. Perhaps in retrospect my want-to file really came from remembering Madear's 1970s brown and golden flowered plastic photo album of her want-tos. I'll always cherish and remember her fondly.

I am moved by the thought of knowing that while I felt alone, I was not alone. There is a history of women in my life who lived the best life they knew how to in the midst of illness, grief, silence, and loss, and somehow that encourages me too. I continued to do what I was learning to do: take my medication, see the therapist, and continue building my want-to file, hoping that at some point my want-tos would come to life in me.

PAUSE TO REFLECT

The following are a couple of steps to reclaiming your want-tos.

- Take some time to reflect on the things you imagined for yourself as a child. It can be helpful to hold a picture of yourself as a small child and ask the Holy Spirit to stir up your desires from childhood that are stored in your memory. Write them down as they come to you. This can be an ongoing process of discovery.

- Consider starting your own want-to file folder or use the various apps and sites like Pinterest that allow you to create an electronic version of the want-to file. Simply begin by capturing images, words, and phrases that seem to capture your attention. They may well be clues to jump-starting your imagination and allowing you to tap into creativity and new life-giving possibilities. Beauty can inspire us and has the capacity to increase our endorphins, our God-given, feel-good hormones that aid our mind-body-spirit in recovery, so by all means add some beauty to your want-tos—perhaps artwork, a postcard, an image from a magazine, or a picture of a beautiful scene in nature.

Interlude

HIKING A MOUNTAIN

I felt that God was telling me, even nudging me—a solid-fist-in-my-back kind of nudge—to do some things just because I *wanted to* and had the power or desire to. One of those things was to join my Renovaré friends Margaret Campbell, Richard Foster, and Richard's son Nathan Foster, who were hiking one of the mountains in Colorado. My response to Margaret's invitation was "I have always wanted to do that." I was in the midst of the crash at the time I agreed to the hike. Thank God I had some time before the hike would commence the following year. Spring would come—May to be exact—and it would signal amazing change.

God had been saying that I needed to walk. At the time I was just too exhausted, but the seed had been planted. I began to walk in preparation for the hike, nothing overwhelming at first. The more I walked the more the walking not only disciplined my body and strengthened me, but it helped to regulate my feeble mind. A month went by and I was joined on my training journey by my mother-in-love, Mildred Rasmus. She unknowingly held me accountable for the exercise with her frequent calls to confirm that I was up and ready to walk. Also Joe Phillips, a member of St. John's who is a professional personal trainer, took me on as a client. Joe is a no-nonsense kind of guy—ex-Marine, strong, and tall—who takes his training seriously. He walked with me and tenderly encouraged me as I worked to get my body in shape and to get my mind back as well. Sometimes he used humor; other times he preached back sermons he had heard me preach. He always knew when to be tough and when to ease up. He became an incredible support for me, some mornings calling me to say, "I'm here waiting on you!" Joe developed a more extensive training program to better prepare my body for what I expected would be a grueling hike. But more importantly he became a strong friend and companion on my journey to recovery, and for that I could never repay him, but I am asking God to.

Finally, on July 17 at 6:15 that morning I met my traveling companions Margaret, Richard, and Nathan at the trailhead of Quandary Peak, near Breckenridge, Colorado. All along I had been anticipating an 8,000-foot climb, only to find out that morning that Quandary Peak is 14,000 feet above sea level.

Okay! O—kay! At that point on my journey I no longer wondered why this mountain was called Mt. Quandary. How ironic. I knew the altitude would be the biggest challenge to overcome, especially because I was coming from below sea level living in Houston.

Our hike began with prayer for safety and favorable weather, which was a threat based on the previous evening's storm. The view was wonderful: Fraser firs with pine cones, aspen trees, blue spruce, and fallen trees that were host to a variety of new life forms. I felt invigorated by the beauty, and being in the vast open space allowed me to feel as though something in me had come alive again. The crisp, fresh air, the gentle breeze, the amazing sky. I felt like singing "The hills are alive with the sound of music." I had never seen such majestic splendor.

Richard suggested that we pace ourselves, so I began what I believed to be an easy stride. I have always walked faster than most people and have judged others by how fast or slow they walked, believing that a fast pace indicated a successful life. Richard added, "Don't worry if people pass you on the trail. Set and keep your own pace. You are not competing with them." How wise of him to offer this novice such solid wisdom.

My companions and I were always visible to one another and in the beginning were able to hold light conversation. But most of the time speaking took too much breath, and we all understood that.

On the trail I was passed often, sometimes with a "hello" or a wave of the hand from a fellow hiker. I had to quickly decide to avoid being intimidated by the pace others had set for themselves.

The timberline proved a training ground for the rocks on the trail. Whereas light conversation was possible on the dirt trail, silence was necessary on the rocks. Some would pass me, and I would yield the way. It was not just courtesy; it was a matter of mutual safety.

A father and son, strangers to me, took a special interest in me. They had already climbed five mountains that week. They reminded me to drink water. Thinking of them, I am overcome when I reflect on God's deep love for me all along my journey. The father and son also encouraged me to rest as needed. Rest was something I never really valued. Rest meant a missed opportunity in the marketplace. Yet rest was what I had heard the Spirit of God tell me a year prior to the crash.

The father, whose name I don't remember, mentioned that there are two approaches to the journey. I could move more quickly and stop, or I could move slowly but surely. He went on to say that he and his son preferred the quick way. By the time I started again I could not see my party at all. I began to realize that if I went a little more slowly, I could maintain my breathing even better. The Spirit gave me the phrase "Slow and easy," and that encouraged me.

The initial rocks were nothing in comparison to the higher level of rocks at around the 11,000-foot mark. The air was thin. Still, I could not believe how much peace I felt, though I could not see my companions.

The higher-level rocks, the "rock scramble," were larger than the rocks at the lower levels and more difficult to navigate. Footing had to be sure—these were the rocks twisted ankles and broken bones were made of. Perceiving my need for direction through the scramble, Richard reappeared to help me pace myself through the new challenge.

"Take your time," he advised. "Keep your feet moving, even if in baby steps. Breathe in on one step and out on the next." Balance and concentration were key.

At that point making the summit was not important; getting through was my only concern. Once through the most difficult part, I came to a clearing, and my companions were there waiting for me. It was not our destiny to summit Mt. Quandary that day. Hikers who had passed us on the trail were returning from the summit with reports of thundering storms and lightning, not a good sign. So wisely, Richard had us turn and go back down Mt. Quandary for the sake of safety.

I have had a "can't wait to get to the top" mentality for most of my life instead of doing the real work of living in the present moment, whether that meant confronting my fears or just determining my sure footing. How many times have I heard the phrase "when we all get to heaven"? Jesus proclaimed that the kingdom is here and now. The opportunity for pleasure and excitement is here and now. Want-tos will not wait forever.

I can't allow myself to be paralyzed by my unsure footing. Neither can I allow the anticipation of heaven to anesthetize me from the reality of this step or the next step on my journey.

Even though I walked through the rock scramble, I didn't have to fear any mishaps, for Richard was with me, his hiking stick and his voice comforted me. Both the absence and the presence of my companions along the way reminded me that "the race is not to the swift, nor the battle to the strong" (Ecclesiastes 9:11 ESV). The race is not given to the swift but to those who endure to the end (see Matthew 24:13). Those words brought to mind the story of the tortoise and the hare, and as I reflected, the Spirit reassured me that it was okay to be a tortoise along the way.

In his book *Streams of Living Water*, Richard Foster writes of Dorothy Day, the social-justice activist and journalist: "This love of all things natural awakened in Dorothy yearnings for all things Eternal. She was happy, blissful. And out of sheer joy she began praying once again, praying her gratitude and thanksgiving." So while we didn't summit Mt. Quandary that day, I, like Dorothy, was awakened one step at a time, tortoise style. And I too found myself praying with gratitude and thanksgiving.

12

SKYDIVING

At the Cenacle Retreat House in Houston, years before the crash, I was introduced to labyrinth walking—the practice of walking a circular path prayerfully and attentively as a means of connecting to God. There were numerous labyrinths in the Houston area, and I found great solace in walking meditatively in this way.

I walked the labyrinth at St. Luke's Methodist Church in Houston many days after taking the girls to school. I came to be still and contemplate God, and I never left disappointed. I recall once inviting Pastor Yvette Tarrant, a friend and colleague, to join me in walking the labyrinth. As we prepared to leave the labyrinth, I heard the Lord say, "Watch your step." That was all I heard, and I didn't really ponder it much. However, when Yvette and I walked to the intersection of a four-way traffic signal, I saw the pedestrian crosswalk light change, and I stepped into the intersection, only to be hit by a driver who apparently had not seen us. Yvette screamed; I was shaken but unharmed, though the woman's black bumper left skid marks on my pant leg. She never stopped to assure my safety. Yes, I have a history of praying and hearing God when I walk the labyrinth. In that place where so many have prayed, something in me always sensed God as fully present to me.

The labyrinth at St. Luke's has at its center a grand old oak tree that stands inviting and strong. On one particular morning after the crash, I nestled under its expansive awning. I felt so loved and supported. God was present as Amma, God as mother to me that morning, and this majestic tree served as a visual reminder. In many ways it was a magical moment. The breeze was cool and welcoming, the sky clear and filled with light. I took a deep breath, and it was as though at that moment I was home.

Settling in on a nearby cedar bench, I heard God. But I almost couldn't believe what God said, the message was so clear and succinct: "Go skydiving."

I felt a rush of adrenaline flooding my being. I've clearly heard God say a number of words in my life, words that encouraged me or words I shared to encourage someone else. But I had never heard God say anything that incredibly exciting. What a contrast to how deflating it had felt as a child to hear my grandmother's words of caution against my earlier attempts at my version of skydiving. What if God was in the adventure? What if God *was* the adventure? What if the adventure was a way toward freedom?

Not My Wife

Early in our marriage I told my husband that I wanted to go skydiving. His response: "When the girls are forty, then you can go." I only imagined that it was said jokingly.

Sometime after that, and after former President George H. W. Bush had gone skydiving when he was in his eighties—an event on every news station and on the front page of our city newspapers—I mentioned it again. It had given me newfound hope. Rudy's new response: "As long as you are the mother of my children you can't do no shit like that."

So, hearing God clearly and distinctly say, "Go skydiving," was unimaginably freeing. Something in me that seemed to have been sleeping as unto death awakened. I felt a rush of joy hearing God give me permission to do something I had longed to do all of my life. I felt as though something extraordinarily wonderful had happened at that moment. Surely I was glowing. All I needed to validate the experience was for the angels to sing the "Hallelujah Chorus."

Just as quickly, however, I thought, *Who is going to tell Rudy?*

I exited the labyrinth slowly, with an awareness of great freedom on the one hand—God Almighty, maker of heaven and earth, had said I could go skydiving—and on the other, trying to be okay if Rudy said I couldn't go.

It was a long ride home.

That Monday morning was our day off, so I decided to simply share my experience at the labyrinth with Rudy. I would not work to convince him on this one. I would keep it short, sweet, and to the point.

As I walked into the kitchen, Rudy asked, "How is your morning going?"

I said, "I walked the labyrinth after I dropped the girls off at school, and God said, 'Go skydiving.'"

Rudy's whole demeanor changed from slightly sleepy, adoring hubby to cold and confrontational all in an instant. The first words out of his mouth were, "Why would you lie on God like that?" His words shocked and surprised me; I couldn't believe that he had accused me of lying on God. I hadn't expected that response, not really. Mind you, this was the same man who had always valued my prayer life. For example, I remembered an incident that happened before we were pastors. We were in real estate sales together. Rudy had a niche market during the early 1980s selling real estate that banks and financial institutions had foreclosed on in and around the Houston area. One particular morning after my quiet time I drove to our office, and I got a message from God. When I walked into the office I told Rudy, "God said buy real estate." He immediately began to purchase property, much of which was in his foreclosure portfolio. He purchased one particular piece of property for five hundred dollars, and we sold it ten years later for fifteen thousand dollars. The sale of that property helped us meet some of our family expenses after we transitioned to working at St. John's full time, where we served for a number of years without compensation. We wouldn't have survived financially had we not bought and sold real estate as God instructed. This was the same God Rudy was now challenging me about now that the subject was skydiving.

I told Rudy, "That is what I heard, but if you don't want me to, I won't go. I think it could be enough satisfaction for me simply knowing that God said that I could." I decided to cease conversation at that point, at least about skydiving. My daddy taught me that it takes two to argue. But all day long Rudy tried to start the skydiving conversation again. It really wasn't a conversation, though, because I had chosen to stay out of it.

I knew my husband had to keep talking about it to process it. So I said to myself and God, "God, you and Rudy work it out and let me know how it ends up!"

Rudy later told me that when he experienced fear, he catastrophized. After being told about me skydiving, all he could see was me falling tragically to my death.

Once again, I was dealing with someone else's fear. I had never considered the possibility of disaster. In my mind there was no greater way to die than in pursuit of something that really mattered to me. We were all going to die anyway. Why not have fun doing it?

Late that Monday evening, Rudy finally came to me and said, "Okay. Go skydiving, but just don't tell me when you do it." Perhaps he had moved beyond his fear to some measure of acceptance.

When Rudy scheduled an out-of-town trip, I called my sister and invited her to be my skydiving guest. She said yes!

Moving Beyond Fear

On the morning of our skydiving date, the sky was clear and radiantly blue as we arrived at the Rosharon Skydiving site. The staff at the hangar was welcoming, and I felt like a little kid tiptoeing into the office to pay my fees and then to the classroom for four hours of preflight instruction. I was on cloud nine. Heck, I could have flown unassisted in the classroom. I was reminded of how I'd felt so free when I jumped from Madear's front porch for the very first time.

As we entered the plane, the roar of the engines seemed to say, "Let's go!" I was partnered with an instructor who reviewed the steps for communicating with each other. He was a serious instructor, but I could tell that he loved his job.

The plane gained altitude, and we moved into position for our jump. I had no idea what I should expect. I felt giddy, so childlike and free, and so very present to the moment. The air rushing by the open door could be heard, and I was euphoric, joyous, and lighthearted even at the anticipation of our jump. I was thrilled to be in that plane. (Dare I say exuberant?) All these feelings arose within me, the good kind I had stuffed all those many years, and they flowed like wine at a party.

Finally, we jumped.

I was in awe of the sheer beauty of the day. Everything about that morning seemed radiant. I had not anticipated the weightlessness I felt and the feeling of being held in the arms of God as we glided on the air's stream. There was no roller-coaster experience as I had imagined, only the feeling of gentle soaring the way eagles do so effortlessly. The silence was palpable, as though it enfolded my entire being. Though we had launched into the sky, there was no plummeting, no uneasiness at all. I was transcending limits, and I had never felt this secure and protected all my life. I felt at one with everything and everyone around me. I felt God speaking the language of love, pure love, out of the deep spaces of silence.

The instructor signaled for me to pull the cord. The beauty was so hypnotizing, the bliss so enchanting that I had forgotten to pull it.

I have spoken to other pilots who have been skydivers in the army and such, and those who loved the experience had a twinkle in their eyes. They had felt the sense of being one with God that skydiving allowed.

Now when I see birds dancing across the sky in their formations, I am reminded of the sheer joy I felt simply because I did something that I had longed to do.

PAUSE TO REFLECT

What have you longed for, wanted to do? Write it down. What would it take to make this want-to a reality? How might your want-to be God inviting you into an experience of freedom?

How might you create an experience that allows you to move beyond limits that you or others have set for you?

How often have you avoided asking for the desires of your heart because you were either afraid or attached to the possibility of rejection or the "no"? What possibilities could you have passed up? What would it take for you to move some things up on your bucket list and start planning to activate your desires? My father created the acronym "DINGOYA—Do It Now, Get Off Your Asset." I'm praying for your courage (or whatever it takes) to move into your want-to!

If you are so inclined, please go to my social media pages and let me know what you are moving up on your list or something that you will be implementing out of your want-to file. I'd love to hear from you.

Instagram: @juanitarasmus
Facebook: @Juanita.rasmus
Twitter: @Pastor_Juanita

13

SILENCE

The Place of Being

*M*any have come to the dark night out of crises of countless sorts: divorce, financial disaster, death of a child, career loss, or devastated dreams. Some come to it through one illness or another or, like me, through the door called depression. The dark night of the soul is the place where one is invited into a deeper, more transformative relationship with the divine. It is the place that, when all that had been our life no longer serves us, lures us, or compels us, we find ourselves void of any identity that matters, with an emptiness in us that longs to be filled. Yet the reality is that none of the old filling will suffice any longer. The dark night is the way into the spiritual depths and oneness with God.

In all of its loneliness the dark night is often filled with deep silence, and the silence too is a significant gift. Commenting on the work of the dark night by Saint John of the Cross, American monk Thomas Keating has said, "God's first language is silence. Everything else is a poor translation. In order to understand this language, we must learn to be silent and to rest in God." While the night is indeed dark, it is poised with spaciousness for hearing the voice of God.

My friend Marie Novack remained present to me as I groped my way through the darkness all those months after the crash. She was partially spiritual midwife by being present and available to me as I sought to birth my authentic self. For years Marie trekked to the desert retreat center Lebh Shomea House of Prayer at Sarita in south Texas. When Marie invited me to do a road trip with her for some silence and solitude, I jumped at the opportunity for a fall getaway.

Solitude at Lebh Shomea
(a journal of feelings and silence)

Marie and I arrived today around 11:40 a.m. She will be in a hermitage, and I am in Judith. I like this room; it has a great balcony porch overlooking the grounds, which are just a lil' honey brown due to the drought that we have experienced in all of Texas this year. Nevertheless, I am grateful to be here again. I lay down after unloading my things from the suburban. I awakened around 4:18 p.m. As usual I am tired. The first thing I heard as I asked God what I needed was "rest." Last night Rudy and I hosted the "Amazing Faith Dinner" for Interfaith Ministries. It was a really delightful evening. Our guests were unknown to us except for Melvin Grey and his girlfriend, Virginia Beauchamp. We had such a warm time that they easily could have been still gathered. Anyway, rest I will.

The dinner bell just rang, so I'll grab some veggies for dinner. It's "fall back" for daylight savings time, and it is black like nothing you've ever experienced. This old Southern mansion is positioned to maximize the sun exposure and provide natural sunlight. And when there ain't no sun, there ain't no light! So, I thought while there was a lil' light that I might need to find the hall light switch and turn it on. Good thinking, Sherlock! It is so dark that you can't see your hand in front of your face. The darkness is just one of the gifts that is here at Lebh Shomea. The darkness has at times forced me to retire at a decent hour and at other times it has forced me to confront my demons.

As I walk down the increasingly dark stairs for dinner, I feel that I may be working on my demons on this trip. I feel so much anxiety and then I walk onto the basement floor and catch a glimpse of Father Kelly eating in solitary. Looking in the dining room I glance over the guest list. It's a ritual of mine, because so often I've come here only to find that someone I know is also on retreat. So, it's kind of neat to be surprised or not, as is the case this time.

I prepared my salad in the silence. Father Kelly came over to greet me, and he was getting a hug whether he liked it or not. My anxiety demanded it, and my lil' Juanita always responds with deep longing at how much he reminds me of a white version of Papa, my mother's father, my grandfather, who lived to age ninety-four. Father Kelly and Papa both are about the same height and have a very similar demeanor and build. They share a love for a good Stetson hat as well. Papa didn't talk a lot, and many of my fondest memories of him are being in the kitchen in the silence or his sitting on the front porch after a long day at work, quiet and reflective.

Papa had been a cook in Galveston for some company—I don't recall which one—and so he did the cooking and grocery shopping, not Madear, who was a stay-at-home housewife. Papa could cook anything, and with great love. Often his meals were very simple, but like the meals here at Lebh Shomea they were made with attention and care. I loved how Papa would slice wedges of cheese and sit silently in the kitchen eating cheese and saltine crackers, or drinking a cup of hot perked coffee, the kind that let everybody near the open kitchen window know that coffee was on. Anyway, I hugged Father Kelly and then took my seat. As I settled myself from the overwhelming anxiety and the sense of just how much I missed having my grandparents around, I begin to tear up and say my grace. Somewhere I heard that anxiety is often about feelings we don't believe we have permission to feel.

Welcome to the next five days at Lebh Shomea. The morning mass was in the Children's Chapel, as it typically is during the week. I noticed the echo during mass unlike ever before. I imagine that it has always been there, but for some reason today I heard it distinctly. The Gospel reading was from Luke 20:27-35 (NRSV). It was the passage where the Sadducees, who did not believe in resurrection, questioned Jesus. They posed a "what if": What if a man marries and has no children and his brothers all marry his wife after their deaths, leaving no children? Whose wife will she be in the resurrection? And Jesus said in essence that eternal life will not look like the lives we have crafted in this day. I love the fact that Jesus always points to the fact that there is another way of living and being that we are clueless about, all the while constantly pointing toward the way that leads to eternal life, the real life. It makes me wonder what stupid questions and selfish motives I would have brought to a conversation with Jesus. Would I have allowed my need for acceptance and approval to have put me center stage of fool's-dom? Or would I, like Mary, just sit at Jesus' feet and take it all in, silently allowing his truth to rearrange my thinking in the secret places of my heart?

I brought the three green little Scriptures that Gregory (Helen) Love gave me at the dinner Thursday night. It is, he says, part of his ministry to pass out little Scriptures, and they have a compelling question on them. Why was I given three? I wonder. He said, "I'll give you three," and he did. I just casually glanced at them and decided that I would bring them with me to ponder in the silence and golden beauty here at Lebh Shomea.

First: Acts 16:1-2 What Will People Say About You?

Second: Jude 1:20 Can You Build on Your Foundation?

Third: Deut. 28:1-14 Do You Act like You Believe This?

Here at Lebh Shomea I am residing in the room called Judith. As I was walking up the stairs from breakfast, I heard the Spirit say go left. I turned to see a few books out for pick up from the library on the first floor. Behold there is the book Judith. I opened the flap, and it describes Judith the saint written of in the Apocrypha, the Catholic section of the Bible that some Protestants aren't familiar with.

I also have a ritual of discovering for whom the rooms are named and a bit about their life, so it is pretty cool to see that I am sleeping, listening, and having my being in a room named for a "deeply religious" and yet murderously cunning female shero.

It came to me this morning during mass that extended times of solitude and silence have the same impact as marinade on tough meat. The marinade begins to gently break down the tough muscle that would be difficult to enjoy during a good meal. Likewise, solitude and silence break down the tough issues in my heart that would make it difficult for Love to abide there if they remained as barriers to God's love. As I wept this morning—not sobbing, just a tenderizing that I and God knew about—I felt gratitude once again for this ministry here in the Texas desert. This is a ministry of tenderizing tough places so that "todo pasa solo Dios basta." *Everything passes. Only God remains. I wrote:*

Silence

Here to hear

Reverberating thoughts

Pace the cell of my mind

Cloaked only in noise.

I sense

the awakening

of my soul.

Fears buried arise

Feelings bound set free

Unfettered

Drop like needless weights.

All inside work

Now I hear, here.

Marinating in God's Presence

Silence is amazing. It's like a marinade to put on chicken, fish, or beef. There are times when I'm like the fish in marinade, easily overcome by the silence. Other times I'm like the chicken marinating; I have to be turned and evenly resting in the silence on all sides because my skin has to be penetrated. Then there are the times I'm like a brisket; I need a longer time in the marinade so my sinews are tenderized and opened to new possibilities. I heard a chef say that a marinade changes the biological structure of the meat it is contained in.

Okay, Lord, marinate me in your silence so that I'm transformed into something fulfilling, life-giving, and memorable. Isn't that what marinades do? This extensive time in silence has revealed so much to me. I have been given time to be with things. Time to be with my own awareness of how I have been driven by my childish beliefs and how those beliefs have created a side of me that is manipulative, especially with my children and those closest to me. I always presumed that my need for their hair to be perfect and them to be well groomed was because I wanted what was best for my girls. You know the need for a good public appearance in a world where our skin already is a strike against us. This kind of manipulation is very subtle. In the silence the nuances of my personality have been revealed for what they are. I needed my girls to look good for me. I saw them—their appearance, their Southern politeness, their civility, their good grades in school—all of this I am seeing now as a reflection of me. In my mind these were the outward signs that would portray me as a good mother. All of this is rooted in my childhood desire for acceptance and the need to please the authorities, whoever they were. I can see now after marinating in silence all these many months how that made me crazy, especially if I was stressed from church life, and that craziness bruised my girls. The curing in silence has revealed this. I pray that I am able to make amends to them for my behavior. I want them to know just how wonderful they are. Each of them has her own brilliant gifts and dynamic way of being in the world. Each of them has

taught me something about seeing the world more vastly different than I ever could have had they not been in my life. Each
of them has taken my heart, my fears, and my hopes and helped
me to see the treasure from the trash. Isn't that what relationships are supposed to do for us? They broaden our senses, deepen
our compassion, widen our range of insight, and lengthen our
ability to become more human because of our encounter.

Marinating has allowed me to see that my daughters have
been incomparable teachers to me. All too often I have seen the
heaviness of disappointment, the shadow of rejection, and the
weight of perfectionism they have felt by my unmarinated corrections, instructions, and unending opinions. Early on I took
them to a child therapist for kind of a mental health checkup,
and I was terrified when the therapist said, "These girls are too
happy, too compliant. Don't worry, we'll get to the root of this."
I grabbed my girls by their tiny little arms and flew like the
Peggy Parish character Amelia Bedelia out of the office and
headed for home! What the hell did she mean they are too
happy and too compliant? The black momma in me justified
that in this brutally white world they must be compliant or it
could mean their lives. Then to question their being happy, oh
my God, that was not what I expected. Quite a good deal of
time has passed since that visit, and I can only wonder if perhaps
I should have stayed. I'll never know, but I am a momma who
has made mistakes along the way.

Sadly, I had no training manual, just like my parents before
me. We have all simply done the best we knew how at the time.
My hope lies in remembering that the Twelve Steps say that we
always have the power to make amends. If I hadn't been marinating, thanks to the crash, there is no telling how much more

damage I may have done to their souls. Marinating in the silence is allowing me to see me. This is heavy shit, but I don't feel punishment, which is what I've always expected in these moments. I feel regret, remorse, and a bit disoriented by my new awareness, but believe it or not I also feel a great deal of gratitude. I believe that when we see something, then we can say something, change something, make atonement. I have the chance to make things better with my girls for the sake of the deep love and respect I have for them. I heard Christiane Northrop say on a PBS special that when a woman does her healing work, she can change the trajectory of the lives of the women in her legacy for seven generations. That gives me hope. I am learning to offer apologies to my girls and to do my correction work both with them and in therapy. I'll be the first to admit that I have a long way to go, but I'm good with that.

Marinating in the silence has helped me to see *me* so clearly, and it has tenderized my heart in such a way that I long to repair the damage I've done. My girls bring me such joy. They are warm, loving, funny, caring, creative, intelligent, fascinating, compassionate, and two of the most loyal kids I could have asked for. They are little girls who deserve an awakened mother to be the bumper for the challenges that they no doubt encounter outside of our home. I want to be their safe space, a place where they can gently, compassionately, and wisely be loved, nurtured, and supported. So, I'm marinating in the silence, and I'm poignantly aware of the deep transformation that the silence is working in me.

I have felt that the depression that started all of this journey was absolutely the worst thing that could have happened to me. At times I have said I wouldn't wish it on my worst enemy. Yet

I feel the warmth of the tears that have begun to roll gently down my cheeks. They are witnesses to my truth that God is in this and that I can feel God's love even here. The suffering is a reality to me here, but so too is the awakening to what is and, perhaps most hopeful, what can be.

Be Still and Know

The Renovaré Bible defines *solitude* as "the creation of an open, empty space in our lives by purposefully abstaining from interaction with other human beings, so that, freed from competing loyalties, we can be found by God." This is what I'm feeling: open empty space, and it feels like home. Renovaré's definition of *silence* is "closing off our souls from 'sounds,' whether noise, music, or words, so that we may better still the inner chatter and clatter of our noisy hearts and be increasingly attentive to God." Here I am experiencing no demands, no competing thoughts even, a kind of bliss. The silence and darkness, the solitude, have guided me to new understanding of what Jesus has been saying to me all this time: "Be still and know I am God." Between the silence and the solitude there is rest, and I am so grateful that I am aware of this now. I am so empty inside that I'm conscious of all of these subtleties. I had to descend all those days and nights into the darkness or I never could have known this ground of my being in God. Isaiah 30:15 says, "In returning and rest you shall be saved; / in quietness and in trust shall be your strength" (ESV).

In this silence I get it. Richard Foster has often said, "Busyness is not of the devil; it is the devil," and the devil had me playing into his hands for as long as I believed that my identity was in my doing. In the stillness I am conscious; I am awake to my being. I know this may sound far-fetched, but I can sense myself beyond my body, my form; here I know that I am presence, energy, life, and light, and I am surrounded by love.

PAUSE TO REFLECT

I have found the following new practices train me to engage with silence.

- Every morning I engage in a meditation practice for thirty minutes. I find that the meditation time has greatly minimized my anxiety. I use several apps that help me, including the Insight Timer, Calm, and the YouTube video "Maranatha Meditation." Start with just a couple of minutes daily, morning and evening, and then build up, as you are able, to twenty or thirty minutes. Most instructors suggest thirty minutes as optimal. Focus on your breathing as a means of being present. One key is to do what you are able right where you are, no judgment, no punishment. Be gentle and kind to yourself.

- Take a power break of silence for five minutes in the middle of your day. Set a timer, accept no interruptions, breathe, and pause. Enjoy the silence.

- Many of us have become so used to noise. What might it be like to drive without the radio? Or to discontinue sleeping with the television playing? Where in your life are there other sources of noise that might be limited or minimized in some life-giving manner? The adjustment is a process, so start small and work up.

- Minimize television, social media, and engagement with email outside of standard office hours. Some have found that while they thought checking their social media was a kind of break from the day, it really was an added stressor, fueling anxiety and the like.

- Make space and time for the Spirit of God to teach you. Lectio divina is a lovely practice that invites reflection and presence. (See details on this practice in chap. 6.)

- Try being quiet for three minutes. Notice what you are feeling, sensing, any awkwardness. Journal out of the silence.

14

IT'S THE THOUGHTS THAT COUNT

I was taught that attitude determines your altitude. Indeed, I have eaten, slept, and drunk the Kool-Aid. I know that my attitude creates the perfume of my existence. If my attitude is foul and negative, the universe gives me back all that I send out. When I'm hyped up and excited, the universe—those around me and those around them—responds. It is all about our thoughts and the energy they create. In his book *Letting Go: The Pathway of Surrender*, Dr. David Hawkins talks about the ability that science now has to observe and calculate levels of consciousness. Every thought has energy, and the closer the thought is to Christ's consciousness, the more positive the effect on us, mind, body, and spirit. A person who is considered jovial, compassionate, and authentic has energy that those around them pick up on, and that person is often considered pleasant to be around. Likewise, people tend to want to avoid a person who is a constant complainer, never sees the bright side, and is perhaps greedy and inconsiderate. Our thoughts create our existence, our lives, and our experiences.

I'll always remember my first trip to New York City about twenty years ago and how excited I was. Prior to going, I frequently told people about my approaching travels. It amazed me how often I was told by this or that person, "You won't like New York! The people there are so rude. New Yorkers are always in such a hurry! Don't try asking for directions. You'll be on your own!" I didn't recall hearing such negative feedback about a city before. I wondered if the folks in New York knew of their bad reputation.

Upon arriving in New York, I was astonished by the energy of the city. It was jam-packed with people. When I couldn't locate the building I was headed to, I walked to the corner and asked a gentleman for directions. He kindly obliged, pointed the way, and even walked me down the block to make sure I saw where he pointed.

I made it to my meeting with time to spare. As I headed back to my hotel, I did what we Southern girls do: I spoke to people when we made eye contact and sometimes received a smile and a gracious nod in return. So far I had not met the rude New Yorkers I had heard about back home. I loved New York. It's possible, though, that I was experiencing the benefits of a good attitude. It must have been all those years of drinking positive-attitude Kool-Aid my dad gave me as a kid. My father knew that our thoughts create our attitude and that our attitude creates our life. He loved to remind us, "As a man thinketh in his heart, so is he or she." Thanks, Daddy, for giving me the heads-up on the power of positive thinking.

Singing in the Key of Life

One thing the crash made very clear to me was the need to get back to the basics. I mean, my mind was totally shut down. I couldn't remember a positive affirmation if you promised to pay off my mortgage. But I had help getting back to the basics, thanks to Louise Hay. Proverbs 18:21 says, "Death and life are in the power of the tongue" (NRSV). The tongue and our thoughts make for the engine of every life. In her book *You Can Heal Your Life*, Louise included an incredible chart filled with affirmations depending on what was going on with your body physically. Depression has its array of physical symptoms, so I selected three of them based on my symptom of the week and came up with this set of affirmations:

- I love, accept, and approve of myself.
- I trust the process of life.
- I am safe!

My grandmother always told me as a kid that an idle mind is the devil's workshop. So these affirmations could give my mind some constructive support to rebuild with.

I wrote my new affirmations on an index card and on my mirror in the bathroom with a dry erase marker. Then it came to me to put them to a song to make it easier to remember because that part of my brain needed prompting and a tune would probably do the trick. I remembered hearing that music therapy has been shown to aid the brain in recovery. I wondered what tune I could use because my memory was still a little depleted. Then I heard "Jesus Loves Me." I was so grateful to God for digging that song out of the mush of my memory!

I began singing the affirmations to "Jesus Loves Me": "I love, accept, and approve of myself, and I trust the process of life. I love, accept, and approve of myself, and I trust the process of life. Yes, I am safe. Yes, I am safe. Yes, I am safe because the Bible tells me so." That works. That really works! I've known that song since I was knee high to a duck. I can remember the affirmations by adding them to this tune that has been in me forever. I prayed, *Thanks, Abba. This gives me some kind of crazy hope. I'm not even sure where it's coming from, but I'm so grateful. It's as though I feel lighthearted all of a sudden, relieved.*

Thoughts Matter

I was in my chair staring into space about nine months after the crash, and I heard the Lord say, "Take yoga."

I welcomed the thought at the time. I hadn't ever considered yoga, not because I thought of it as weird or anything but because I thought of it as exercise. I never really get up for regular exercise like that. I do enjoy dancing, but the kind when the song comes on the television or pops into my head and I instantaneously decide *I'm gonna dance!*

Anyway, as I considered yoga a thought popped into my head: *What if Sharon finds out?* The notion of my mentor, Sharon, finding out struck me with such intense feelings of humiliation, I suddenly felt vulnerable and judged even by the thought of her possible reaction. Sharon is traditional and somewhat narrow in her theology. With its Eastern spiritual roots I couldn't imagine she would be open to a Christian practicing yoga.

With all the silence that I had been living in since the crash, I found that my deepest feelings tended to rise to the surface without any filter or warning. It was as though my defenses had all been worn down, so when I thought of something that had feelings attached, those feelings came up and out. Marinating in silence for all those many months was exposing emotions I had stuffed away for far too long. I finally had the space to pay attention to them instead of going on autopilot to seek and destroy them, instead of normal responses like "ain't nobody got time for all that!" In the days immediately after the crash I may not have felt much. But at this point on this journey, my feelings were coming to life in a big way. So, my thoughts about what Sharon would think had my feelings shooting up with the force of a missile. It was maddening to see how clearly that idea sailed into my consciousness, yet I couldn't stop wrestling with that question.

I don't recall ever being that conscious of wondering what other people thought about a decision I was making. But in an instant I saw how invested I had been in a way of thinking that had literally controlled my life. I have the silence and stillness to thank for that awareness; they pulled the covers back and showed me my reality. I was exposed—to myself. It felt surreal, yet I was so aware of the presence of love and the sense that it was time for me to see that stuff. If it hadn't been for the comfort and acceptance of God that I was feeling, however, that would have been totally overpowering.

For some reason I had imagined my thoughts and actions were pretty much my own, but I saw so unmistakably how "what will other people think?" questioning had been going on in the depths of my being, and that was scary as hell to me. I, all of a sudden, felt unimaginably vulnerable. It's one thing to talk about our thoughts affecting our actions, but it was happening in real time and I witnessed it, like seeing a car wreck that had just happened.

One evening shortly after the yoga incident I tuned in to the local public television station and heard Wayne Dyer talking about being a witness, without judgment, just noticing our thoughts. It sounded reasonable, especially with my concern about being judged for practicing yoga still lingering in my heart and mind. It was troubling to realize that I had been harboring thoughts of other people's opinions and judgments about me. Now, if it had been Rudy or my girls, that seemed distinctly different because I loved them and valued their opinions. Yet as I sat there, the awareness was crystal clear: this wasn't a new pattern but was simply the first time I had been present fully to my own thoughts. I have heard people say that they were afraid of silence. I get it now! Because of the silence and slowing down, my thought life became magnified to me. It was almost overwhelming, but I wasn't paralyzed by it; I was made glaringly aware. This was the me I had not wanted to see.

A few years after the crash someone gave me a small card with a litany called "The Litany of Humility" by Rafael Cardinal Merry del Val. This litany came to mind, especially these selected compelling lines:

O Jesus! Meek and humble of heart, *Hear me.*
From the desire of being approved, *Deliver me, Jesus.*
From the fear of being humiliated, *Deliver me, Jesus.*
From the fear of being despised, *Deliver me, Jesus.*

Reading this litany was like steeping a tea bag in hot water. The longer I steeped in its words, the more it revealed.

I am amazed at how often I had operated out of fear and desire to please without even knowing it. Now it's as though a small video is running in my mind of all the sermons I had prepared and unconsciously wondered what this person or that person might say. How many times had I prepared a workshop or Bible study or worn a certain outfit, all with the weighted unconscious thoughts of longing for someone else's approval or wanting to be praised or preferred?

Awakening to my thoughts has been one of the most profound gifts of the crash, yet it felt wretched and distressing in the beginning. I had never made the connection that my thoughts were so deeply rooted in fear and my need to be preferred, the teacher's pet as it were. That awareness remains alive with me. I don't feel hopeless, but I feel the remorse of having squandered a lot of time and energy in the wasteland I was calling my life. It was as though I had eaten something that I had eaten a thousand times before, but this time it burst into flavor, exploding in my mouth and sounding alarms the way hot peppers might. Taking the time to be with my thoughts has been transformative.

I promised the Lord that I would go to the YMCA for yoga as soon as I could get the energy to get out of my chair. Not long after that, I did attend yoga.

PAUSE TO REFLECT

There are so many symptoms that can come with depression, including body aches and pains and sciatica (also known as a "pain in the butt"). Louise Hay's *You Can Heal Your Life* is great in providing healing affirmations and profound awareness of possible root causes in our thinking that have facilitated the physical distress. We might ask ourselves, for example, What is going on in our life that is a pain in the butt? Whatever our answer, we are invited to work on that place. It's not uncommon to feel like our body and mind are at war when experiencing depression. I believe they are warring for us to live in an authentic way, a way that gives us new life. Jesus called it the abundant life.

The *raisin meditation* is a profound way to take something we've eaten probably an untold number of times and use it to experience new awareness. The meditation invites us to be present to the raisin as if for the very first time, being a witness, without judgment, just noticing our thoughts and experience of the raisin. You need a single raisin and five minutes for the experience. It will be helpful to read through the meditation and have a journal before you begin the practice.

SEEING. With clean and dry hands hold a raisin between your thumb and finger. Just look at it, notice it, take note of what you are seeing. What are you aware of as you put your attention on the raisin? Notice the ridges and valleys. How does the light reflect on it? Note any features you observe.

TOUCHING. Roll the raisin gently between your thumb and finger. Closing your eyes while you do this may help sensitize you to the experience.

HEARING. Bring the raisin to your ear and shake it. Listen for any sounds as you gently roll it between your thumb and finger.

SMELLING. Allow yourself to take in the smell of the raisin. Breathe it in deeply, as though you were smelling it for the first time. Is there any aroma, fragrance, or scent? Notice if smelling the raisin affects any other part of your body, such as your stomach or your mouth.

PLACING. Without chewing, place the raisin in your mouth. Notice how your hands and arms cooperate out of familiarity (our thoughts are the same way). Using your tongue, press the raisin to the top of your mouth and hold it there. Now move the raisin with your tongue to the right side of your inner cheek, still without chewing it. Notice the sensations that are occurring.

TASTING. Move the raisin to the left cheek and slowly, with great awareness, begin to chew it. Pay attention to what you are experiencing without swallowing. What sensations are occurring in your mouth? Are there any memories that come to mind? Notice the moment-by-moment changes occurring as you enjoy eating the raisin.

SWALLOWING. Be present to the desire or intention to swallow the raisin before you actually do, then swallow.

FOLLOWING. See if you can follow the raisin as it moves into your stomach. Notice how your whole body may be responding now that you have meditated on the raisin. What came to mind for you while you did the meditation? What memories may have come up? How will you remember this meditation?

How might God be inviting you to pay attention to your thoughts? How might the remembrance of this practice aid you in being present to God's guidance, correction, and insight into your thought life? Take a moment and reflect. Write out your thoughts and awareness. How might you become a witness, without judgment, just noticing your thoughts as Wayne Dyer suggested?

15

DOING . . . DOING . . . UNDONE

We began our work at St. John's the way we did everything: we worked *hard*! Rudy and I are both entrepreneurial, and we know how to scrub floors and shake hands. We did whatever needed to be done, which was a lot. Stepping onto the property it was clear that we were being called to serve the needs of the least of these, especially the homeless who found refuge on the doorsteps at night.

We rotated the preaching and shared the responsibilities. It was a workaholic's paradise. I taught two Bible studies a week, and Rudy managed the homeless services and administrative "wrangling," as he calls it, for which he is better suited. Rudy doesn't suffer from a need to please or to be accepted and approved of as I do. Rudy delegates well and sets boundaries.

Seven years later I looked up to find that the nine members had grown to three thousand. St. John's had become a dynamic congregation with incredible needs and too few hands to help.

We simply worked harder. I don't think either of us realized the toll the growth was taking on us physically, mentally, or emotionally—until the crash. After that I believed that my pastoral ministry was over. I was ready to call it quits; I just didn't seem to have the stamina.

Lazily Working Hard

Dear friends of ours, Katherine and Dred Scott, gave us a copy of Eugene Peterson's book *The Contemplative Pastor*. Bit by bit, word by word, I could hear the wisdom of God speaking. Eugene said:

> I am busy because I am lazy. I indolently let others decide what I will do instead of resolutely deciding myself. I let people who do not understand the work of the pastor write the agenda for my day's work because I am too slipshod to write it myself.
>
> The pastor is a shadow figure in these people's minds, a marginal person vaguely connected with matters of God and good will. Anything remotely religious or somehow well intentioned can be properly assigned to the pastor.
>
> Because these assignments to pastoral service are made sincerely, I go along with them. It takes effort to refuse, and besides, there's always the danger that the refusal will be interpreted as a rebuff, a betrayal of religion, and a calloused disregard for people in need.
>
> It was a favorite theme of C. S. Lewis that only lazy people work hard. By lazily abdicating the essential work of deciding and directing, establishing values and setting goals, other people do it for us; then we find ourselves frantically, at the last minute, trying to satisfy a half dozen different

demands on our time, none of which is essential to our vocation, to stave off the disaster of disappointing someone.

His perception was painful, but not more so than my recovery. While I did not use the word *lazy*, I was indeed relinquishing my power and authority to others.

Eugene didn't pull any punches, and his straightforwardness jolted me to attention. I like that about him. I needed clear and candid insight. I simply had been doing too much without any healthy boundaries, but I had been clueless. I was serving as a pastor, marketing person, member of various committees, and women's ministry director, all while playing supermom and superwife. It was too much. But I didn't know any better. I did what needed to be done. I was working *hard*.

Eugene had my undivided attention. I continued to read as he outlined my call, and it was a breath of fresh air. He defined the role of the contemplative pastor as one who *teaches*, *preaches*, *prays*, and *listens*. And I realized—Oh my God, that's me!

Eugene helped me to see when I am living my best life, when I am nourished and full and charged for living. I need silence and solitude to listen for God's guidance. I now know that I'm best when I'm teaching, preaching, praying, and listening. These four areas make life rich for me, fulfilling and life-giving, joyous, not laborious, depleting, and downright hard. Peterson's words made it clear to me that I was co-creating a new life with God in a way that I had never understood before. I love the way he translated Colossians 3:3-4: "Your new life, which is your *real* life—even though invisible to spectators—is with Christ in God. *He* is your life. When Christ (your real life, remember) shows up again on this earth, you'll show up, too—the real you, the glorious you. Meanwhile be content with obscurity, like Christ" (*The Message*). No wonder the clarity was so life-giving for me; it was rooted in Christ, and teaching, preaching, praying, and listening had always been pivotal for me. Now I was clear that these were the spaces I had to cultivate and curate in ways that were life-giving for my own soul's sake.

Doing Again

Several times in the months after the crash, I got dressed, put on my happy face and lipstick, and made it to the front door of the church on a Sunday for worship services but had to turn around and head back home because I became panic-stricken at the church entry. There were numerous times when I felt that I was ready to return to my life and work. My disposition seemed better, I felt stronger internally, and my physical aches and pains seemed to have diminished, so I believed I was good to go. After six months or so, I was eager to get back to things as they had been. I had gone from lying prostrate in bed to sitting up and taking nourishment by mouth. As my cousin Dennis would say, I wanted meaning. However, I didn't realize that unconsciously that meant a return to my old way of doing.

That time was kind of like when a person takes the seven-day antibiotic pack that doctors prescribe. By the third day they feel pretty good, but by the fourth day, they're going stir-crazy. So the person goes back to work and winds up exhausted. It was too much too soon.

I loved teaching Bible study and preaching. I needed somewhere to engage life again. But my ego wanted life as it had been. I began to move into my typical ways of going about my life— only to be hammered by relapses.

Nine months after the crash, I started to garden and take in vitamin D—a necessary vitamin often lacking in people living with depression. I also started to regain my interest in my husband and the girls, which meant I could sit on the sofa instead of lying on it when they came home from their day. Since I felt stronger, I decided to take the girls to school again as well as take a few household responsibilities off Rudy's plate.

During that time, Rudy and the girls basically had gotten suckered in by a new car salesman who talked them into getting in a dark green minivan while he took Polaroid pictures of them and adhered one to a card that said "Congratulations" on it. Next thing I knew, my family had come home with a card, a lovely picture, and a hideous minivan. They dragged me outside to see the "surprise." They were all so exhausted by my condition and knew that I loved surprises.

I really think the minivan was their attempt to get Mommy up and rolling again, just like when Rudy and the girls painted our kitchen and breakfast nook neon orange and yellow. I knew that too was an unconscious way of turning my light back on. I dearly love my family for this.

When I realized that I could recognize humor, it was the best day in a long stretch of not-so-good days. I remember the day well, as it was our inaugural trip to middle school in the dark green minivan. The radio station was tuned to our favorite station Majic 102.1—KMJQ FM. The station had supported the Thanksgiving food drive of our nonprofit ministry, Bread of Life, for years, so naturally that station was near and dear to my heart. Besides, they had a great morning drive-time show, "Funky Larry and the Morning Crew," that was hilarious. Prior to the crash, I had enjoyed the show crew's riotous take on life and our world.

Needless to say, I hadn't laughed in months, nor had I been listening to the show since I was bedbound. But that morning Funky Larry said something hilarious that made me smile. I hadn't smiled in months. This was the first time in a long time that I had felt something alive in me. Immediately I noticed that the corners of my mouth ached from the movement. It was like the feeling people have when leaving the dentist's office after having had to keep their mouths open during a lengthy dental procedure. My mouth literally hurt from a small church-lady smile. At that moment I realized that all this time depression had taken my smile away. No wonder my family painted neon colors in the house and bought the gross green minivan "surprise." They had been living without my smile all that time. Living without me all that time. That thought made a tear roll down my cheek.

Depression steals joy, light, and laughter, but not just from you. It robs those who most love you of what they love in you. Even now I feel sad about that, knowing that Rudy and especially my babies had to live in this darkness with me. Still, I'm grateful—not for their having had to cope with this but that I can actually feel the sadness I hadn't felt for so long.

I hadn't felt anything for so long. Surely, it was a sign: *I'm awakening again.*

My life was starting to shape up. Or so I thought.

A New Start

That sense of awakening energized me and seduced me into doing more. I felt stronger. The few things I had done hadn't left me drained. I was finally comfortable driving again. While the thought of going back to the church was still too much to handle,

I wanted to do something with my time. I even found a special place to volunteer—an organization that provided support to adults with learning differences—one day a week for a couple of hours before I picked the girls up from school. I had noticed the building as I drove by it, so I parked the car one day and went in to investigate. It felt like I had walked into Santa's workshop.

The coordinator introduced herself. When I told her that I wondered if they needed volunteers, she jumped on that question like white on rice and introduced me to the program and to the students. They were loving and so receptive.

As per Rudy's request, I was careful. He didn't want me to jeopardize my recovery; understandably it had been as much his recovery as mine after all. So I volunteered by helping to paint the ceramics the organization sold to support the craft program for the adult students.

Some of the students were nonverbal and others clearly childlike in their communication, but if I tell you I felt loved when I walked in, believe me, that would be an understatement. This was just what I needed—a place to contribute but not in a demanding way. Here I was able to exercise a little paint-by-numbers kind of creativity while being present to the warm glow of light that filled the studio and the joy of the students who focused on their own projects.

I looked forward to my weekly visit. The students would greet me, some with rough grunts and sounds, others with short greetings like those of very young children. I felt welcomed and appreciated. My painting in the studio felt contemplative; there were never any difficult decisions to make, and the community around me felt life-giving after spending so many months at home alone during the day. This was just what I needed—

enough interaction without any real conversation to speak of. Once I entered the room and greeted the students, it was basically silence except for some conversations between students that might as well have been music in the background for me.

After a number of weeks of volunteering, I got the bright idea that perhaps I could return to worship service. One Sunday morning I got up, dressed, and left long after Rudy and the girls so I wouldn't be obligated to stay for all three services.

I felt some excitement as I approached the church and parked the car. At the entrance several of the greeting team members called out greetings. But as I headed toward the sanctuary, I was flooded once again with a tidal wave of anxiety, as though I might do something foolish. I panicked and felt vulnerable in a way that I couldn't explain, and I had to leave. All I could do was get out of the church, back into my car, and drive home as quickly as possible.

I remember back in high school having a drink at a friend's party. The father had made the drinks, but I simply didn't drink like the white kids I went to school with. The margarita was so strong that after a few sips I felt panicky and sat in a chair for the rest of the party. I'd had enough sense to know that I could possibly say or do something crazy.

After I returned home from the church, I climbed into bed. I was grateful that I had made it out without incident. I had felt so alive. What went wrong?

Relapsing on Doing

My first therapist, Pittman, told me in one of our sessions, "Juanita, you will have to live with this for the rest of your life." At the moment I wanted to scream, "How dare you condemn me to this!" But this relapse helped me to see what I couldn't hear from him.

The body can recover far more quickly than the mind and emotions, its energies rebounding after substantial rest, proper nutrition, and care. On a cellular level, new life is being regenerated. But though I felt stronger and more alert, I felt the way a rubber band might feel (if it could feel) after having been stretched to its maximum capacity but suddenly finding itself at a state of rest. I simply wasn't ready, but I didn't know it.

I know now that the ego wanted me back on the streets, as it were, so it could regain its power over my being. It was cheering for my return like a pimp roots to keep prostitutes on the street at all cost. My ego was all too eager to get me back into the ruts created in my mind over a lifetime, the same ruts that had landed me here. However, the ego is a maladaptive taskmaster—it knows no other way to rule. So, in the confines of my home I'd get all psyched up about how well I felt.

Relapse is no joke.

I have known relapse in several ways as I have been on the journey toward being. Relapse comes from feeling so much better that you mistakenly believe you no longer need the medication. Before my own diagnosis I had observed numerous relapses among people at church. Back then, I could never quite figure out why they would stop taking their meds only to spiral out of control and have to regain the same ground in recovery all over again. Now I know: the ego and the desire to be "normal" and return to our old self is a tape that plays so doggone loud that we find ourself acquiescing to the need to get on with life. The question I asked myself is, which life? The same life that got you here in the first place, Juanita? Or are you willing to take the long, slow road toward building a life that you can live with?

We are so programmed to do what we know, what is familiar, no matter that the last letters in *familiar* are *liar!*

Even now, as I write this book, I struggle to remind myself that recovery is a process, and no one has a recipe that declares I am done. I am not a Thanksgiving turkey basting until the peak of golden-brown goodness, glistening through the oven window suggesting that I am ready. Recovery doesn't work that way. So, relapse reminded me that I had to take my meds and take my time and allow my mind, my thought life, my will, and my emotions to catch up to my body. It's a delicate balance trying to gauge what the new normal is and when is the right time to return to the fast lane called life. I keep affirming for myself that I am choosing to go it slow.

Rudy often said to me, especially early in the recovery process, "Juanita, remember to use your low beams." His words were our code that I need not enter any space with my high beams on, that my light is light whether it's a spark or a torch. There were times when I could spark fairly easily, but anything more required a great deal of energy that too often landed me back on the sofa in a horizontal position.

Recovery is like a dance: two steps forward, one step back. I have never been good with following dance instructions, and I've learned now that it's okay. I can choose one day at a time—heck, sometimes it's one minute at a time. Slow is my new normal.

PAUSE TO REFLECT

In *Healing the Purpose of Your Life*, authors Matt, Sheila, and Dennis Linn coined the phrase "Meaninglessness makes you sick, meaningfulness makes you well." We have been given the power and authority to claim our meaningfulness, or, put another way, to take our power back. In her ebook *Women and Personal Power: The Way It's Been Taken from Us and How We Can Get It Back*, author and therapist Sandra G. Moore gives a history of women and how structures over time have diminished our sense of personal power. Hers is the work of retraining the mind and soul, offering some much-needed guidance and opportunities for deeper self-reflection as well as practices to support the new way of being. The cases she mentions make the experience all the more real. Though I have only just begun this new way of perceiving my meaningfulness, this book is noteworthy reading. Moore has been known to say to her clients "claim your deserving"; this too is part of the work of recovery.

We have the right to "claim our deserving." It starts by taking a good, long look at the way we have been showing up on the job, in our relationships, or in the world. The crash gave me space for a long look. Reflect over the past thirty days. Have there been spaces where you simply had too many demands on your time, energy, and resources?

Four questions came to me. Though "invisible to spectators," they were inviting me to be with myself and my new life. Ask yourself,

- Who am I really?
- What do I need now?
- What do I really want?
- What gives me life at my core?

We are all told of the necessity of an annual physical exam, but I am promoting a monthly checkup from the neck up. Ask yourself one of the questions repeatedly for thirty seconds (set a timer if you like). Then record every answer that is revealed to you without judging or condemning it. The subconscious is like a wild animal in the woods. We must be quiet and still if we want to catch a glimpse of it. After thirty seconds, jot down the insight and/or words that came to you. Then take the next question. By marinating our minds with the question repeatedly, we move deeper into the space of the truth. Give yourself permission to be in the woods of your being and to hear what truth may be revealed. How might your insight inform your new way of thinking and being in your world?

What makes your life meaningful and purposeful? What keeps life rich and full for you? If no one has asked you that before, your want-to file might offer some insight. What gives you joy?

16

IT'S ALL GRACE

*E*ver read certain terms in the Bible and wondered whether or not you had experienced their fruit when you needed them most? *Grace* is one of those words for me. It's always been a bit elusive, difficult to really internalize to me. The crash allowed me to see that my whole life had been consumed with striving for acceptance, pushing toward greatness before God and all those other authority figures around me. I often felt that God's grace was for those who were really catching hell in their lives, and at St. John's there was never a shortage of folks struggling with this or that dilemma: struggling to keep this child out of prison or to keep the lights on or to keep the car running. I heard countless struggles, real or imagined, so I always had a kind of barometer. My little problems never got to the disastrous level. So as long as I believed that I could control my situations, I didn't think I needed to use up my portion of grace or "unmerited" favor. That kind of thinking was still deeply rooted in not feeling worthy or accepted or that I had to earn grace. I have come to realize, however, that *grace* is simply another word for *love*. John Main said it well in *Silence and Stillness in Every Season*: "Indeed it is a grace that we should be seeking to be open to the supreme reality that is God, that is love. . . . Do not try to unravel the mystery but allow God to unfold His mystery in your heart. God will do so within the simple union of love you have in the deep centre of your being."

I can honestly say that I am grateful that my mind and body did for me what I could not do for myself: they shut me down, stopped me dead in my tracks. No dramatic scenes, no crazy making in public. Just a phone call to babble that I wasn't going back to the church, that I needed a sabbatical or something. Then I lay down in bed for what felt like an eternity, unable to get up or out.

The Proverbs 31 Woman Revisited

At the end of chapter four I included an interlude on my reaction to the Proverbs 31 woman. In the silence and stillness of my recovery, I have had to come to terms with her. She is more real to me than ever before.

King Lemuel's mother taught him this acrostic poem celebrating the value of a virtuous wife. No doubt she shared her wisdom in hopes that she might steer her son toward a rewarding life as king, a life that included having the "right" kind of wife. My parents modeled Proverbs 31 really well for me. They lovingly showed what grace and fidelity in marriage look like and what it means to be industrious and loyal.

My father fit the image that King Lemuel's mother suggested for her son: responsible, wise, and faithful. My mother has been the virtuous wife: diligent, supportive, creative, and caring. Their roles in my life have been invaluable. They found and lived into a way of being with enduring composure. I can see grace operating in the fullness of their lives together.

I was living into my own way of doing it all, spinning full plates because I thought this was the way to be virtuous. How is it that the Proverbs 31 woman had gotten what she wanted, but when I tried to use her example, all I got was depressed?

I heard Peter Rollins, the Northern Irish philosopher and storyteller, say at a concert in Houston that "depression is sadness for not getting what you want. Melancholy is sadness for getting what you wanted." Nowhere in Lemuel's ode is there any indication that this woman was dissatisfied with her life. Neither was I, on the surface.

Even as I drifted slowly across the words of the poem, I sensed a kind of ease, energy, and aliveness that made it possible for her to live her life well. I had never noticed this in her before. My perspective was so skewed. I now find in her freedom that I do not possess even today, but it is in sight. She orchestrated all that she did out of a more wholesome place than I have known. I, on the other hand, have usually worked out of a place of striving that left me no room for the spacious ease, a rich spontaneity of life, freedom, or joy.

And yet in the depths of the solitude of my depression, I had grown to feel more alive than I had known since childhood. Even a year after, the recovery seemed sure, more real, more permanent, like being on solid ground emotionally. I wasn't turning cartwheels—I never knew how—but I felt as though a five-hundred-pound monkey had been taken off of my back and I could finally breathe again. It was as though my mind and soul had been cleaned out, the way you can turn on your oven's self-cleaning mode and walk away while the cleaning gets done. Now, years after the crash, I realize I had gotten so many ideas about living so wrong. I believe I got this woman wrong too.

I had believed this poem was the picture of a day in the life of this woman. I have come to see that the poem is a summary of her life. She knew her seasons of life and did what was appropriate during those seasons. She wasn't trying to run for "Most Outstanding Wife," "Most Exceptional Mother," "Most Skilled Pastor," or any of the like. I don't sense that tension at all, only freedom and autonomy as she chooses her fabrics and selects her purple.

When I was a child, I watched my mother select cloth at a fabric store. There was no rushing, only silence and intense concentration on the fabric as though my mother was unaware that my sister and I were even present. She was in a sacred zone, a space of creativity and being. She would comb through row after row of fabric, gracefully touching, totally present to the experience. She was a skilled lioness on the hunt, silent and still lest she miss what she had come for. I sensed anticipation in her that she would find what she sought. When we left the store, my mother had an expression on her face that I can now describe as pure joy.

Being cloistered in my home gave me time to reflect. I had seen the Proverbs 31 woman's way of living as a life summed up in her accomplishments—in essence, her doingness. I believe differently now. In my mind she values silence and stillness maybe in the early morning or perhaps late at night when her home and heart are quiet. She lays out her desires before God, and the two of them co-create her days and ultimately her life.

There is no "hurry up and wait" in this woman's life. She makes time for her servant and lives out of the wise counsel God provides her. This is how grace flows like sweetness in her life. She knows that God's grace is present for her, seen and unseen. She creates space for grace to be revealed. Out of the sweet awareness of grace she knows she need not fear for her household, for it has been secured by pure love.

What I Learned About God

I have suffered so much anxiety because I thought I was responsible to create, sustain, guide, and direct. You know, what the mind can conceive and believe it can achieve, right? But where does the power come from to support what the mind is conceiving, believing, and overachieving?

I grew up reciting Philippians 4:13—it has been my charge to live by. I had always believed that when the text says, "I can do all things through Christ who strengthens me" (NKJV), the underlying implication is that I am able to do *all* things, *period*. I didn't know I had the freedom to say no or ask for help to discern whether *all* was my assignment. I was working for God like Lucy and Ethel on the conveyor belt (see the interlude after chap. 4). Not until now have I understood that "all things" means those things that fall within my realm and in my season. Now I understand that every good thing to do is not necessarily mine to do right now.

All too often my inability to pause and allow God to speak to me and guide me meant that I said yes before considering the cost of my yes. My agenda, my beliefs about my life, and the ways that I had been seeing God literally locked out my ability to perceive the ways of God's grace.

I had long been shattered like Humpty Dumpty. It is by God's grace that all the king's horses and all the king's men couldn't put me back together again. Had I been put back together by people, it would have meant reliving the same old ways of doing and thinking about myself, my life, and my God. This brokenness has been a grace in my life. I was running on foolish fuel. I discovered how my own thinking had boxed God out and, as a result, had boxed me in to an unsustainable way of doing life. My old ways of thinking, believing, and doing left no room for grace. God's strength gives me the power to live a virtuous life—a life of being, a life that is filled with joy, contentment, peace, and hope. Not a superficially perfect life, but I think of it now as a real life worth living.

Treasure Found

I found a treasure in the darkness that made the long journey of despondency worth the descent. In the dungeon of depression, I learned the vastness of God's presence and love, like a mother caring for a wounded child. That's the image of the God I found.

In chapter five I talked about the day I lay across the bed, unable to remember how to get out of the bed to go to the restroom. That day was my first clear awareness of God's grace for me. Tears are puddling in my eyes as I write this, tears of gratitude. If I had been able to hop right out of bed that day, I don't know if I would have heard God say what I had longed to hear: "I love you, Juanita. You can't *do* anything for me."

There, in that position, weighed down by the burden of doing until I had been undone, I heard God declare God's crystal-clear and thunderous love for me. It echoed in the hollow of my emptiness. Not only that, God declared that this love was not dependent on my ability to do a gosh-darn thing for God or anyone else for that matter. That day God declared I was more than enough, no matter what the state of my mind, body, spirit, or awareness.

I have reflected on those words, which have become like water to my parched soul. I am loved, and I am treasured. I always have been loved by God, and I always will be. Now I know without a doubt that God loves me. I can feel God's presence in the deepest part of me, especially in the silence and solitude. They ground me in God.

I wasted so much of my life. I was asleep to the reality of life in God, the kind of life John 15 refers to as abiding (NRSV). The spiritual practices help me to keep abiding, to stay in the presence of God, and to know my grounding is through Christ and thus anchors me in God. This life that God has longed for me to know is, as my friend Donn Thomas said, "a life of love, joy, and peace in the Holy Ghost."

I recently reflected on the passage where Jesus was baptized by John the Baptizer: "As soon as Jesus was baptized, he went up out of the water. At that moment heaven was opened, and he saw the Spirit of God descending like a dove and alighting on him. And a voice from heaven said, 'This is my Son, whom I love; with him I am well pleased'" (Matthew 3:16-17). In this text Jesus submits himself to the rite of purification by asking his cousin John to baptize him in the Jordan. Jesus goes down into the Jordan as an act of submission, and as he is lifted up, the pronouncement comes that Jesus is the Son of God, indeed loved by God, and God has found pleasure in Jesus' being. The long days of silence and solitude during my recovery freed me to see that my old way of life had to be surrendered. I had to go down to get up! The old life had its good moments—I will not discount those at all. But I see now that I had built my life on my own and only occasionally opened a window to God's grace and transformative influence on me. I know God was seeking a deeper relationship with me. Now I am so very grateful that I know the robust fullness of the presence of God available to me in the vast hollowness that was the depression.

My life was taken down to the bones. God has breathed new life into me. I, too, feel as though I have seen heaven open and have heard the voice of God say, "This is my daughter, whom I love; with her I am well pleased."

ACKNOWLEDGMENTS

*I*n so many ways my life began when the "good" girl that I was married the boy with the dark cloud over his head. Others saw it. I saw no such dark clouds. I simply knew that I had never felt safer with anyone outside of my parents' home than I had with you, Rudy. I had never felt more open and free than when we were together. Rudy, you opened a world to me that spoke of possibility, promise, and passion. I never wanted to leave your side. You made me feel alive and giddy; we laughed a great deal and shared our hearts and our hopes and in time our hurts. I will always remember the vows my uncle Sam asked us to repeat and accept. "For better or for worse, for richer or for poorer." Those words never felt threatening. Then he said, "in sickness and in health," and he paused as he looked you in the eyes and said, "She's healthy now."

Why the pregnant pause after she's healthy now, I wondered. It wasn't the moment to say, "Uncle Sam, what do you mean?" I was twenty-three-years young and quite healthy, so the comment at that moment seemed odd and puzzling. Years later, I know it was one of those moments when the prophetic voice of God was punctuating the air with awareness.

Rudy, can you believe that was thirty-five years ago? I'm amazed at how time has flown by. We have often reflected on

Uncle Sam's pregnant pause and the crash that followed fourteen years later. There are no words to adequately thank you for not only honoring our vows, especially the "in sickness and in health" part, but for your steady hand of protection on our home and family, and your overarching commitment to faithfully uphold your end of the vows. Thank you for your fidelity. I have fallen in love with you a million times over, having known your love for me and your tenacity for keeping me safe when I was most vulnerable. Thank you, Baby.

Morgan Elena and Ryan Victoria, the two of you are the most beautiful, gracious, loyal, creative, loving, compassionate, tenacious, truthful daughters I could have had the pleasure of mothering. I can't thank you two enough for all the tender ways you were with me during my crazed life in ministry, the crash, and the long days of recovery that followed. You two deserve an award! "Most Supportive Cast."

I now know that when one person in a family system is sick, the whole family system is sick. I shudder to think of just how difficult your lives were, and we did not know how to consider your needs when I was diagnosed. I ask that you would forgive me for abandoning you for my bed and all the other ways before and after the crash.

My prayers are that each of you seeks your most authentic and liberating self. It is worth the investment. I pray as well that you come to know in the deep well of your being whose you are and who you are at your very core. That will make all the suffering worth it if you too will learn to honor your very being!

I love you forever,
I like you for always,

as long as I'm living,
my baby you'll be.

The three of you have been God's gift to me and you continue
to transform the way I live, learn and love.

I love you,
Beda, Mommy

This book has made me keenly aware that books are like children;
they need a village. My heartfelt thanks to Cindy Bunch for
inviting me every year for ten years to write this book. To my
new family at InterVarsity Press who have come alongside me,
thank you! You all are like cousins that I didn't know I had; you
keep showing up, and you all bring gifts.

To all the family near and far, too numerous to name, thank
you for saying, "How's the book coming?" You helped me stay
the course, my deepest gratitude.

I have been so grateful for my companions during the dark
days of the crash: Brenda Chevalier, Carol Bell, Cynthia Briggs
Eagleton, Kirbyjon and Suzette Caldwell, Margaret Campbell,
Sandy Clark (posthumously), Cheryl Creuzot, Ava Graves,
Margo Harris, Byronne Hearne, Carvel Jasmin, Sonny Messiah
Jiles, Tina Knowles Lawson, Terri Ryan, Charlene Slocum,
Yvette Tarrant, others mentioned in the pages of this book, and
all those who prayed for me or gifted me with notes and acts of
kindness, for walking with me along the way toward being. To
each of you I give my thanks. I can never repay you but I am
asking God to.

NOTES

2—Who Am I?

12 *"If you want to find the purpose"*: Myles Munroe, quoted in Paul Excellence, "When Purpose Is Not Known," *BecomExcellence* (blog), accessed October 12, 2019, http://becomexcellence.blogspot.com/2011/01/when-purpose-is-not-known.html.

17 *Byron Katie's "The Work"*: Google "Byron Katie The Work" for free information and insight in to the use of the four questions.

3—The Hollow Bunny Rules

25 *"God brings it"*: St. John of the Cross, *Dark Night of the Soul: A Masterpiece in the Literature of Mysticism*, ed. and trans. E. Allison Peters (New York: Doubleday, 1990), 46.

26 *Byron Katie's The Work*: See "The Work of Byron Katie," https://thework.com/resources.

4—Perfectionism and the Good Girl

27 *Personality Plus*: Florence Littauer, *Personality Plus* (Old Tappan, NJ: Fleming H. Revell, 1983); *DISC:* "DISC Personality Test," 123test.com, updated December 14, 2018, www.123test.com/disc-personality-test.

the Enneagram: For more information, go to the Enneagram Institute's website: www.enneagraminstitute.com.

28 *"motivated by the need"*: Renee Baron and Elizabeth Wagele, *The Enneagram Made Easy: Discover the 9 Types* (San Francisco: HarperSanFrancisco, 1994), 11.

"To this personality type": Don Richard Riso and Russ Hudson, Personality Types: Using the Enneagram for Self-Discovery (Boston: Houghton Mifflin, 1996), 378.

5—*Could I Just Hit Bottom Already?*

41 *"Religious experience"*: Howard Thurman, *The Creative Encounter* (Richmond, IN: Friends United Press, 1972), 40.

6—*Finding My Being*

44 *Renovaré*: See the Renovaré website at https://renovare.org.

51 *I Love Lucy* episode "Job Switching": See "Job Switching," *IMDb*, accessed November 11, 2019, www.imdb.com/title/tt0609243.

8—*What's Anger Got to Do with It?*

66 *"But when knowledge comes"*: Howard Thurman, *The Inward Journey* (Richmond, IN: Friends United Press, 1986), 17.

67 seeing *"for the first time"*: Thurman, *Inward Journey*, 17.

10—*Claiming a New Identity*

88 *"some things are loved because they are worthy"*: Ian Pitts-Watson, quoted in Peter G. James, "Worthy of the Call" (sermon, Vienna Presbyterian Church, November 11, 2007), 2.

90 *"We labor unceasingly"*: Blaise Pascal, *Pensées* (Paris: Librairie Generale Francaise, 1972), 59.

11—*Have-to Versus Want-To*

101 *"Anticipation is a great word"*: Lance Witt, "The Spiritual Discipline of Anticipation," Sermon Central, May 1, 2017, www.sermoncentral.com/pastors-preaching-articles/lance-witt-the-spiritual-discipline-of-anticipation-2861.

102 *"The correct perspective"*: Dallas Willard, *The Great Omission* (New York: HarperCollins, 2006), 12.

109 *"This love of all things"*: Richard Foster, *Streams of Living Water* (New York: HarperCollins, 2001), 159.

13—*Silence: The Place of Being*

118 *"God's first language is silence"*: Thomas Keating, *Invitation to Love*, quoted in Cardinal Robert Sarah, "Silence: God's First Language," *Catholic Thing*, July 7, 2017, www.thecatholicthing.org/2017/07/07/silence-gods-first-language.

121 *"deeply religious"*: From Judith, a New Translation with Introduction and Commentary by Carey A. Moore in the Anchor Bible.

14—It's the Thoughts That Count

131 *Louise included an incredible chart*: Louise Hay, *You Can Heal Your Life* (Carlsbad, CA: Hay House, 2017), 149.

134 *Litany of Humility*: Rafael Cardinal Merry del Val, "Rafael Cardinal Merry del Val," *Wikipedia*, accessed November 13, 2019, https://en.wikipedia.org/wiki/Litany_of_humility.

15—Doing... Doing... Undone

139 *"I am busy"*: Eugene H. Peterson, *The Contemplative Pastor: Returning to the Art of Spiritual Direction* (Grand Rapids: Eerdmans, 1989), 18-19.

145 *I remember back in high school*: I'm not advocating teen drinking by sharing my story, but it was commonplace and a reality that I found out later that had been devastating to way too many of my schoolmates.

147 *"Meaninglessness makes you sick"*: Dennis Linn, Matthew Linn, and Sheila Fabricant Linn, *Healing the Purpose of Your Life* (New York: Paulist Press, 1999).

148 *We have been given the power and authority*: Sandra G. Moore, *Women and Personal Power: The Way It's Been Taken from Us and How We Can Get It Back* (n.p.: Amazon.com Services, 2017).

16—It's All Grace

151 *"Indeed it is a grace"*: John Main, *Silence and Stillness in Every Season: Daily Readings with John Main*, ed. Paul Harris (New York: Continuum, 1997), 169.

152 *"depression is sadness"*: Peter Rollins, opening speaker for a Rob Bell concert at White Oak Music Hall, Houston, Texas, February 20, 2018.

Acknowledgments

159 *"I love you forever"*: Robert Munsch, "Love You Forever," in *Love You Forever* (Richmond Hill, ON: Firefly, 1986).

BECOMING OUR TRUE SELVES

The nautilus is one of the sea's oldest creatures. Beginning with a tight center, its remarkable growth pattern can be seen in the ever-enlarging chambers that spiral outward. The nautilus in the IVP Formatio logo symbolizes deep inward work of spiritual formation that begins rooted in our souls and then opens to the world as we experience spiritual transformation. The shell takes on a stunning pearlized appearance as it ages and forms in much the same way as the souls of those who devote themselves to spiritual practice. Formatio books draw on the ancient wisdom of the saints and the early church as well as the rich resources of Scripture, applying tradition to the needs of contemporary life and practice.

Within each of us is a longing to be in God's presence. Formatio books call us into our deepest desires and help us to become our true selves in the light of God's grace.

VISIT

ivpress.com/formatio

*to see all of the books in the
line and to sign up for the
IVP Formatio newsletter.*